BABYCARE
for
BEGINNERS

DR. FRANCES WILLIAMS

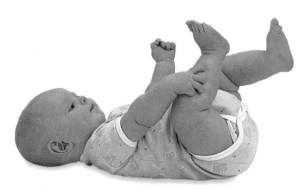

HarperPerennial

A Division of HarperCollinsPublishers

W9-AGK-458

Created and produced by
CARROLL & BROWN LIMITED
5 Lonsdale Road
London NW6 6RA

ART DIRECTOR Chrissie Lloyd

EDITOR Madeleine Jennings
ASSISTANT EDITOR Joel Levy

ART EDITOR Carmel O'Neill
DESIGNER Karen Sawyer

PHOTOGRAPHY Mike Good, Ian Boddy, Debi Treloar
ILLUSTRATORS Christine Pilsworth, John Geary

PRODUCTION CONSULTANT Lorraine Baird
PRODUCTION MANAGER Wendy Rogers

FIRST EDITION
Library of Congress Cataloging-in-Publication Data available upon request.
ISBN 0-06-273104-1
95 96 97 98 99 C&B\TWP 10 9 8 7 6 5 4 3 2 1

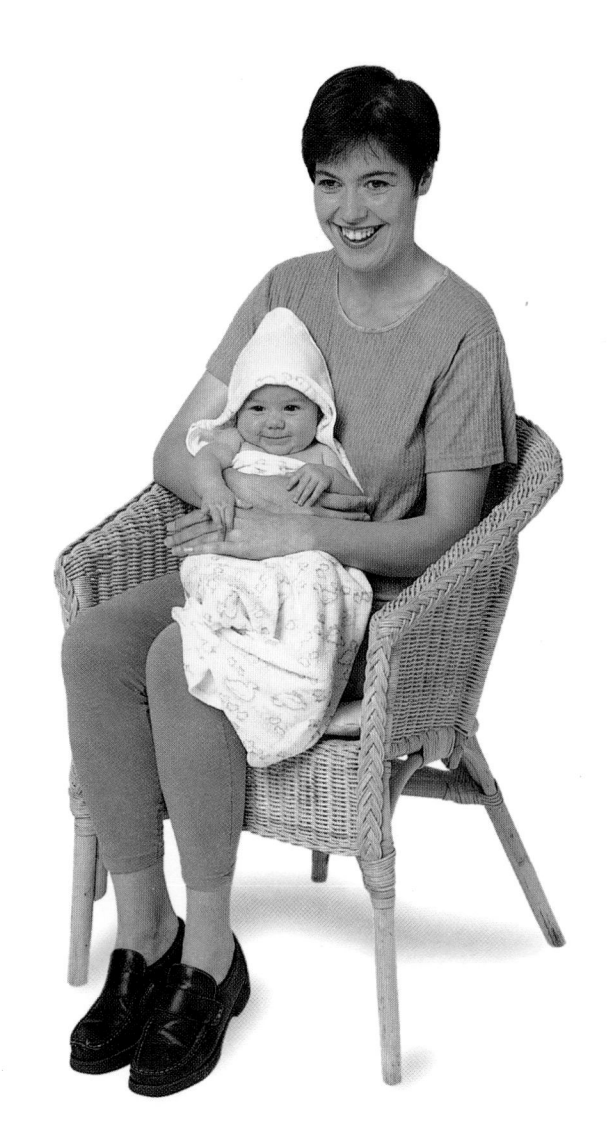

CONTENTS

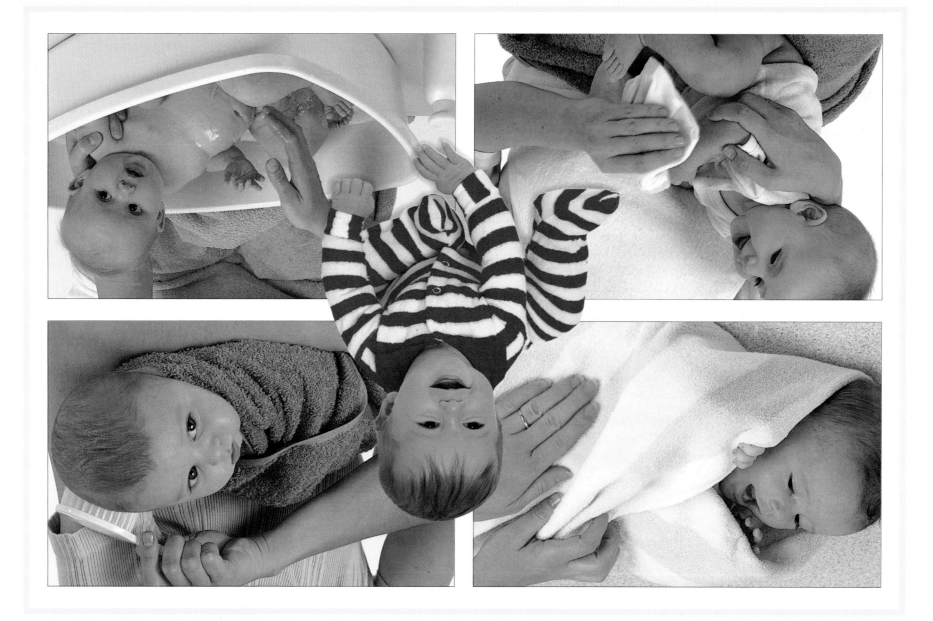

FOREWORD

*O*nce a baby arrives, parents have their hands full. Taking care of a baby is round-the-clock work and a hands-on occupation. Having been carried around for the first nine months of their lives, babies yearn to be in constant contact with their caregivers. Rare is the parent who very shortly doesn't wish he or she had an extra pair of hands when it comes to taking care of a baby, particularly at such nerve-racking times as getting a baby bathed and dressed.

Now help is at hand for new parents and others unfamiliar with basic baby care. Inside you'll find everything you need to know in order to hold, feed, carry, change, dress, bathe, soothe and comfort a newborn baby up to his or her first birthday. And, to do so, you never have to take your hands off your baby at a crucial time in order to turn over or hold down a page. All the necessary information has been designed to be seen at eye level.

Babycare for Beginners *has a unique format that enables it to stand open on a changing surface, dining table or close to the bath, so that you can keep your hands where they are needed – on your baby. Large step-by-step photographs illustrate all the necessary stages of essential care routines such as changing a*

diaper, putting on a jumpsuit, using a baby carrier or preparing a bottle. Large, bold headed captions make following along easy – even at a distance. And when time is not of the essence, there is much useful information contained on the flip side of the pages.

Having shown the early stages of the book to the parents of older children in my practice, the overwhelming reaction has been "We wish this book had been around when we first had our babies!". I know what they mean. Parenting skills are not inborn, they have to be acquired. I hope my book helps new parents, grandparents, babysitters and caregivers gain the confidence and competence necessary not only to care for their babies but to enjoy doing so.

HANDLING YOUR BABY

A young baby needs constant picking up and carrying, which should be done as gently and smoothly as possible. Though a baby is usually more robust than you might think, never shake or handle your baby roughly. When picking up your baby, stay in close body contact, make reassuring noises and support his head at all times.

PICKING UP FROM A FACE-UP POSITION

Your young baby will invariably be placed on his back for sleeping and diaper changing (see Putting down your baby, pages 10-11) so, as a result, you will usually need to lift him from a face-up position.

If your baby is sleeping it is a good idea to rouse him gently before lifting. Until you become practiced at lifting, the motion may seem sudden and startling, which can cause him to cry. Talk to your baby softly or gently stroke his cheek as you prepare to pick him up. To make it easy on your back, always bend down close to your baby before easing him up.

"*I got such a thrill when my son held out his arms. It was almost as though he knew I was about to lift him.*"

1 SUPPORT HIS NECK AND BOTTOM

Lean in close to your baby and slide one hand under his head and neck and the other beneath his bottom. You can approach from the side or from between his legs. A few calm words from you will reassure him and give him a sense of security.

2 GENTLY BEGIN TO LIFT HIM

Still leaning well forward, take your baby's weight in your hands, making sure his head is well cuddled. Talk to him and establish eye contact as you raise him smoothly from the surface.

3 BRING HIM TO CHEST LEVEL

Assume a more upright position and, turning your baby's body so that it is parallel to yours, bring him toward your chest. Try to keep his head raised slightly above the level of the rest of his body.

4 REST HIM IN THE CROOK OF YOUR ARM

As you bring him close to your chest slide the hand supporting his bottom up to support his head as well. Bend your other arm across your body so that you can support his head in the crook of your elbow and his body along the length of this arm. Use your other hand for extra support.

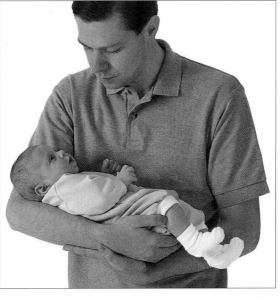

PICKING UP FROM A FACE-DOWN POSITION

Although you will be picking up a young baby from a face-up or supine position most of the time, there will be occasions when you have to pick your baby up from a face-down or prone position, for instance when he rolls forward during sleep. Initially, you may find this maneuver awkward.

THE MORO REFLEX
If your baby starts to feel insecure he may exhibit the Moro reflex. This is characterized by your baby flinging out his arms and legs, throwing his head back and crying. It commonly occurs when your baby experiences a sudden change of position or when he senses he is falling. Doctors interpret the Moro reflex as an unconscious attempt by your baby to regain his balance. There is also a similar reflex known as the startle reflex.

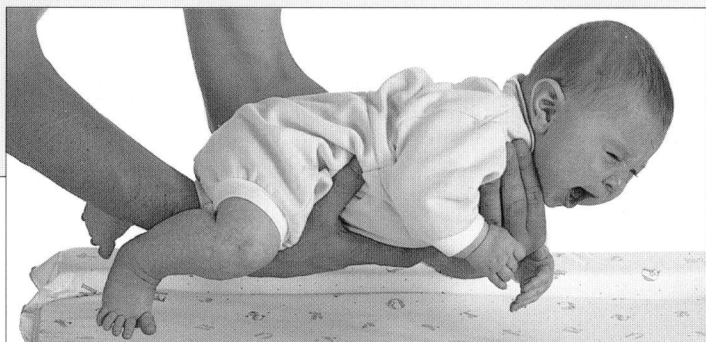

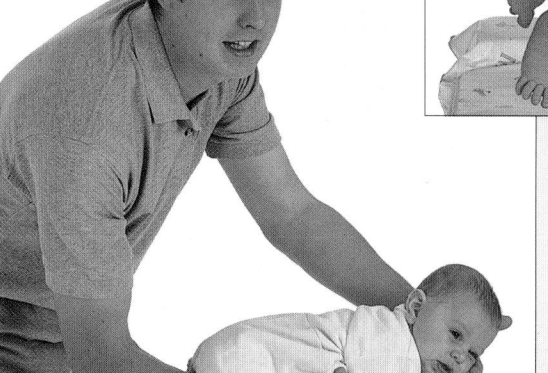

THE WRONG WAY TO PICK HIM UP
When you support a young baby's neck, make sure you keep his head in line with the rest of his body. Don't raise his head further back than the rest of his body (see left) or press too hard on his neck (see above) – you may restrict his breathing.

YOUR OLDER BABY

By about six months of age your baby should become quite adept at rolling from his back onto his front. So, even if you lay him down on his back, he may turn over and you will have to pick him up later from a face-down position.

By this age, too, he also will have mastered the skill of raising his head and chest off a surface. You might like to put him in a face-down position (and therefore pick him up from this position) to enable him to further strengthen his neck muscles. Playing airplanes – stretching out your arms and getting him to copy you – can be fun for both of you.

1 SUPPORT HER NECK AND TUMMY WITH YOUR HANDS

Slide one hand between your baby's legs until your palm rests on her chest. Gently position your other hand underneath her cheek, making sure her head is well supported.

2 LIFT AND TURN HER TOWARD YOU

Slowly raise your baby up, making sure her body weight is well supported. As you lift her up, gently rotate her toward your own body. Keep her head raised slightly above the rest of her body, supporting her head with the crook of your arm.

3 CRADLE HER IN YOUR ARM

As you turn her toward you, put the hand you had between her legs underneath her bottom. Lower your other arm so your baby's head rests in the crook of your elbow, and your forearm supports her along her length.

PUTTING DOWN YOUR BABY

Your baby enjoys the physical sensation of being held in your arms and would happily spend all day like this. However, this is rarely possible. You will certainly need to put your baby down in order to change him or to put him into his crib.

Put your baby down in a relaxed and confident manner. Talk to him all the while so he doesn't sense anything negative or feel abandoned.

Research has shown that putting a baby to sleep on his back or side can significantly cut his risk of falling victim to SIDS (Sudden Infant Death Syndrome) so, during the first three months, you should always put your baby down on his back.

PACIFIERS
Because it can soothe an unsettled baby, a pacifier can be a lifesaver to a harried parent.

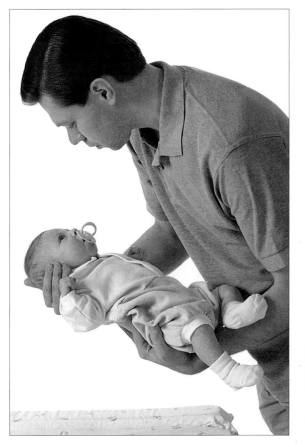

1 GENTLY EASE HIM AWAY FROM YOUR BODY

From a cradling position, gently slide your arms apart so that one hand cradles your baby's head and neck, and the other supports his bottom. Slowly move his body away from yours and over a padded surface.

2 LOWER HIM DOWN

Turn your baby's body so that it is more perpendicular to yours. Bend close to his changing mat or mattress and slowly lower him onto the surface, bottom first.

3 REMOVE YOUR HANDS

After his bottom has made contact with the surface, gently ease your supporting hand from underneath then lower his upper body and head. Keep his head well supported until it is resting comfortably on the surface, then gently slide your hand away.

HOLDING YOUR BABY

All babies enjoy physical contact; in fact they need to be held and caressed to feel secure and loved. As a new parent you will consequently find yourself holding your baby a great deal of her waking hours.

A young baby cannot hold her head up independently, so when you hold her you will need to be careful about supporting her neck.

Your young baby also will feel much more comforted if her limbs are securely held. Your baby has only recently emerged from a tightly confined space – her mother's uterus – so she won't really enjoy the sensation of air on her skin or of being suspended in space. She will want to be held close.

" I loved holding my baby in my arms and being able to see her expressions change. "

YOUR OLDER BABY

Once your baby has gained sufficient control over her neck and can assume an upright head posture, after about three months, she will require less support. There are a number of ways to carry your baby so that she can get a different view of her surroundings.

- ### Nestled against your shoulder
  A baby will be comforted if he is in a position where he can feel your pulse or hear your heartbeat. Use one hand to support your baby's bottom and the other to protect his neck.

- ### On your hip
  Sit your baby astride your hip with her legs either side of your body and support her with one arm under her bottom. Use your free hand for extra support on her back if she can't hold on sufficiently.

- ### Face down in your arms
  Your baby's head should lie just over the crook of your arm with your forearm supporting the length of his body. Put your other arm between his legs so that your hand is resting on his tummy.

- ### Front facing forward
  Hold your baby against you with one arm under her arms and across her chest. Use your other hand to support her bottom.

CARRYING YOUR BABY

Whether you are taking your baby for a local outing or wanting to keep her in close proximity at all times, an infant carrier is the ideal choice. Using one of the many forms available, you will be free to move around and use your hands *to perform everyday tasks while your baby will feel safe and snug. Soft cloth carriers including slings and pouches are ideal for young babies, while older or heavier babies are best carried in more substantial backpacks with aluminum frames.*

USING A SLING

Babies love being held in close contact to the body and a soft cloth sling is the ideal way to carry a very young baby. Your baby will find the movements of your body soothing and will be comforted by the sound of your heartbeat.

Becoming a seasoned babywearer – that is, carrying your baby about in a sling for a major part of the day – involves taking a different approach to baby care. Rather than viewing the time spent holding and carrying your baby as an interruption to your daily routine, try and think of it as normal, with occasional breaks of 'down-time,' when your baby plays or rests in her crib.

Carrying your baby in a sling brings many advantages. Your baby will be easily accessible for you to caress and reassure, and she will find pleasure in your proximity. You will be able to carry out most of your daily tasks without interruption. The majority of parents say that they feel much closer to their children and more 'complete' when they practice babywearing.

Bear in mind that no matter how much support the sling provides, you should always protect your baby's head with your hands when bending forward or to the side. A young baby up to four months of age will also need to have her neck well supported.

For safety's sake, always put the sling on and make sure it is securely fastened before you put your baby inside it; similarly, remove your baby from the sling to a safe place before taking off the sling. Never leave your baby unattended in the pouch of the sling. Don't use the sling to carry your baby while you are driving or as an outer wrap for your baby. After washing, make sure to check that all fastenings remain secure.

BEFORE YOU BUY

▶ Take your baby along with you when choosing a sling, so that you can test it out for size and comfort.

▶ Make sure that the sling supports your young baby's head and neck, and contains her body well.

▶ Check the quality of the material, zippers and any other fastenings.

▶ Make sure the sling is machine washable – it will soon get grubby with frequent use.

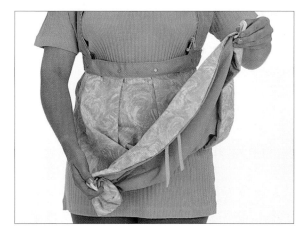

1 PUT ON THE SLING
Following the manufacturer's instructions, open out the sling, attach the straps to your shoulders and fasten the cloth to the waistband.

2 CREATE THE POUCH
Take the hooks – one at each end of the cloth – and attach both to the same ring on one side of the shoulder strap, creating a pouch.

3 PLACE YOUR BABY INSIDE
Gently lift your baby into the pouch positioning her head at the end opposite to where the pouch is hooked. You can raise or lower your baby's position by adjusting the straps on the hooked side of the pouch.

4 CHECK SHE IS COMFORTABLE
It's easy for a baby to become overheated in hot weather, so feel her skin every now and then to make sure she is not sweating.

TRANSPORTING YOUR BABY IN A CARRIER

Cotton, padded and machine washable, baby carriers are one of the most popular ways of transporting a young baby. Most models enable you to hold your baby either close to your chest or facing forward. A young baby will be reassured by the sound of your heartbeat; an older baby will enjoy looking out at new surroundings.

Baby carriers have stiff padding behind the head to give extra support and protection to a young baby who doesn't yet have strong enough muscles to hold up her head on her own. For forward-facing use with an older baby, this padding is removable.

It is very easy for a young baby to overheat inside a carrier as she is held close against an adult's chest. Be sure to dress your baby in light clothing, especially in the summer months. Check every now and then that your baby is not sweating too much or in any discomfort.

BEFORE YOU BUY

Most manufacturers will include a warranty against any product irregularity, but observing the following pointers before you decide to buy will save you a lot of bother.

▷ Check that the stitching is free of any faults. Triple stitching gives the greatest strength and durability.

▷ All buckles, zippers and fasteners should work smoothly.

▷ The shoulder straps should sit comfortably and be well padded.

▷ The fabric should be washable and shrink proof – your baby carrier will soon get grubby with a lot of wear.

PRACTICE MAKES PERFECT
At first, you may find that putting on the carrier is a bit tricky and time consuming. Before you venture out with the carrier, practice putting it on and taking it off at home, as well as putting your baby inside it and taking her out.

REMOVING YOUR BABY FROM A CARRIER
When you are ready to take your baby out of the carrier, sit down, loosen the straps then lean forward as you lift her out.

1 PUT ON THE CARRIER

Following the manufacturer's instructions, fasten the straps and the buckles. When the carrier is secure, then pick up your baby.

2 EASE YOUR BABY INSIDE

Sit down comfortably on a chair. Open out the carrier and, holding your baby under her armpits, slowly lift her into the carrier.

3 CHECK HER POSITION

Guide her feet through the leg holes and lift up the back of the carrier so that the padding supports her neck.

4 ADJUST THE STRAPS

Once she's comfortably seated, check that your baby's weight is evenly supported and adjust the straps accordingly.

5 REASSURE YOUR BABY

When you carry your baby make sure you communicate with her through eye contact and touch. This helps to make the experience enjoyable for both of you.

SOOTHING A CRYING BABY

During the first few weeks of life, crying is the only way your baby can communicate her needs, and she may cry for up to five hours a day!

Most commonly, a baby cries because she is hungry but a number of other situations – discomfort, loneliness and boredom – will trigger this response (see below). A regular caregiver will soon learn to recognize the different cries which can indicate the various causes, but sometimes your baby will cry for no discernible reason. This will no doubt upset and frustrate even the most confident parent, but remember, don't take your baby's crying personally; simply comfort and reassure her with your presence.

It is important that you respond to your baby's cries within a few minutes. The longer you leave your baby to cry, the more distressed she will become. If left to cry, she will become even more upset, making it difficult for you to interpret the original source of her anxiety.

Babies whose cries are ignored become non-responsive as they mature. Be reassured: you won't spoil your baby if you respond to her cries. You will, however, communicate to her that her needs matter to you and that they will be met.

> **" It's amazing how quickly I could distinguish my baby's cry from those of other babies. "**

OFFERING A PACIFIER

Many babies find pacifiers comforting but parents worry they may affect a baby's teeth. In fact, they are not damaging to a child's bite during the first year and most children abandon them more readily than their thumbs. A pacifier should be kept sterile, never sweetened or tied around your baby's neck; nor should it be a substitute for a parent's love and attention.

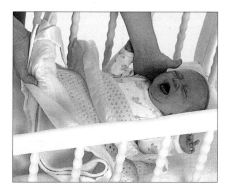

• Is she too hot?

A young baby can quickly overheat because her body's temperature 'control' system takes months to become fully operational. Feel the back of her neck to see if she is too hot. If she is, remove any blankets or a layer of her clothing.

• Is she lonely?

Most babies don't enjoy being separated from their parents. If you cannot be in the same room as your baby, return frequently or talk to her loudly so she knows you are nearby.

• Is she bored?

Your baby may need something to interest her. Even a small baby may stop crying if you give her a toy to play with or a mobile to distract her.

• Does he have a tummy upset?

Your baby may be crying because of gas pains in his stomach after feeding. To relieve this, lay your baby across your knees on his stomach and gently rub his back.

• Is he insecure?

Your baby may need comforting. Sucking is always pleasurable and even though he is not hungry, he may need to feel something in his mouth for reassurance. Offer him a pacifier or your clean little finger.

• Is she overstimulated?

Too much fuss and activity surrounding your baby can be bewildering. Swaddle your baby (see pages 20-21), take her to a quiet room and gently rock her in your arms.

SWADDLING YOUR BABY

Snugly wrapping your baby in a blanket or shawl is a useful technique for soothing and comforting her. After spending nine months in the safe, warm confines of your uterus, being able to freely move her arms and legs can come as quite a shock to your newborn. Through swaddling, you can help recreate your baby's former environment, making her feel safe and secure while she slowly adjusts to the outside world.

Your newborn baby has little control over her arms and legs and any sudden, jerky movements they make can startle your baby and wake her from her sleep. Swaddling can prevent this by keeping her limbs firmly wrapped. You can, however, keep her hands and arms free if she likes suck her fingers.

Swaddling also keeps newborn babies warm while their bodies learn to regulate temperature. However, overheating has been implicated as a cause of SIDS (see page 58) so, if you feel your baby might get too hot, just use a large piece of gauzy material instead of a blanket.

" Being handed a swaddled baby is just like receiving a gift-wrapped present! "

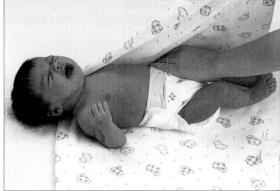

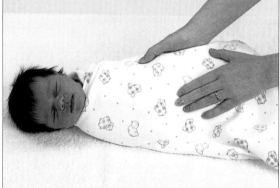

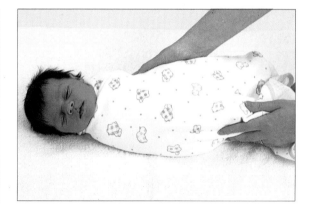

1 POSITION YOUR BABY ON THE BLANKET
Fold a receiving blanket or shawl into a triangle. Lay your baby down in the center so her neck aligns at the top.

2 TAKE ONE END OVER HER SHOULDER
Pull one side of the blanket over her shoulder and diagonally across her body.

3 TUCK THE END IN
Bring the corner under her other arm and tuck under her bottom.

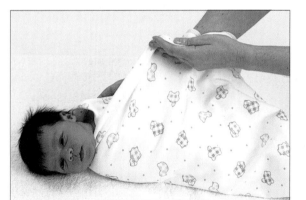

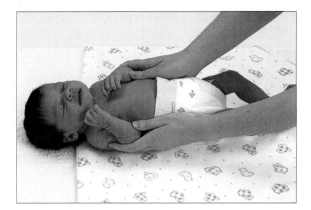

4 FOLD OVER THE OTHER SIDE
Take the other corner and pull it over your baby's shoulder. If you like, tuck her arm up against her neck so she can reach her hand.

5 TUCK THE FABRIC IN
Fold the material neatly under her body so she is held securely. Check that the blanket is not too tight against her neck.

6 COVER HER FEET
Finally, gather the open folds at the bottom and tuck the material underneath to cover her feet. If your baby is not already fast asleep, it's certain she soon will be.

FEEDING YOUR BABY

From nursing or bottlefeeding through to watching your baby feed himself, mealtimes are among the most pleasurable activities of the day. To make them go more smoothly, you will need to learn how to prepare a bottle and solid foods. You will want to make certain that all feeding and preparation equipment is thoroughly clean and that you give your baby foods free of additives and excess sugar and salt. Making your own baby foods can help ensure this.

STERILIZING BOTTLES

If you choose to bottlefeed your baby it is important for your baby's health to maintain a high standard of cleanliness. Milk is the perfect breeding ground for bacteria and if you are not careful your baby could suffer stomach pains and fail to put on weight at a crucial time of his development.

While today it is no longer considered necessary to use special sterilizing solution, all feeding equipment must be kept scrupulously clean. Bottles, nipples, rings, discs and caps must be thoroughly washed in warm soapy water then rinsed clean. The feeding equipment should then be sterilized in a specially manufactured sterilizer, such as the Gerber Sterilizer shown below, or in a large pot of boiling water.

Alternatively, after you have washed all the equipment by hand, you can stack the bottles, nipples, rings, discs and caps in specially designed racks and put them in the dishwasher with a hot water cycle temperature of at least 180°F (82°C). Sterilizing can change the shape of the nipples, particularly the hole size, so check them frequently.

Your young baby will be using up to eight bottles a day, although commercial sterilizers rarely hold more than six; therefore, you will have to plan on doing two loads a day. As your baby gets older, he will make do with fewer bottles, which will make your workload easier, but you should still continue to sterilize all feeding equipment until your baby is nine months old.

TRAVEL TIP
Bottles that hold disposable liners are a good choice when traveling as they don't need sterilizing. The nipples, however, must be sterile. Fill the liners with ready mixed formula for a fuss-free excursion.

YOU WILL NEED

- bottles, nipples, discs, rings, caps
- rubber gloves
- dishwashing detergent
- bottle brush
- household salt
- special nipple-shaped brush
- sterilizer, large pot or sterilizer stacking rack
- sterile tongs
- large paper towels (for draining)

1 Wash bottles
Fill the sink with warm soapy water. Use a bottle brush to wash the bottles, especially the screw thread at the top of the bottle where hardened milk easily can get stuck.

2 Wash nipples
Clean the surface of the nipples then turn them inside out and scrub using a nipple brush. For particularly stubborn milk particles, rub in household salt, which acts as an abrasive.

3 Rinse in clean water
After washing, thoroughly rinse bottles, nipples, discs, rings and caps in clean, hot water. If you can, let the water run through the nipples to check that holes have not become too large.

Boiling method
Bottles can be sterilized with boiling water. Submerge and boil for ten minutes, then let the pot cool while the lid stays on. Use sterile tongs to remove items onto paper towels and leave to drain.

4 Fill up the sterilizer rack
Place bottles upside down in the rack, and discs, rings, caps and nipples in a dishwasher proof glass in one of the bottle slots in the rack.

5 Put rack into sterilizer, cover and switch on
Fill the steam chamber of the sterilizer with water and place the rack inside. Cover with the lid and switch on. Once the water has boiled away the sterilizer will automatically turn off.

MAKING UP FORMULA

Feeding your baby with formula milk is now a healthy and convenient alternative to breastfeeding. Today, there are a number of milk formulas on the market catering to a range of dietary demands, and bottle preparation has become less time consuming and fussy than in the past. Powdered formula based on cow's milk is still the most popular but always consult your doctor about which formula to use for your baby.

There are a few basic rules to follow when preparing formula. The most important is to always make sure your hands are clean and that all the equipment you use is sterilized. Follow the manufacturer's measurements to the rule as they are calculated to suit your baby's needs exactly. Adding too much formula to the water can make your baby sick, while adding too little may result in your baby becoming undernourished.

It is a good idea to make up a number of bottles at one time. This way you can store them in the fridge and take out a bottle at a time as necessary. Always throw away any left over milk.

YOU WILL NEED

- kettle
- measuring jug
- formula
- scoop
- leveling off knife
- stirring spoon
- funnel
- bottles, nipples, discs, rings and caps

1 BOIL THE WATER
Fill a kettle with some fresh water and boil. Let the water cool then measure the required amount into a measuring jug.

2 MEASURE THE FORMULA

Use the scoop provided in the formula can to measure the required amount. Use the flat part of a knife to level off any excess powder.

3 STIR THE FORMULA INTO THE WATER
Add the formula to the water and mix well with a large spoon. Stir until all the powder has dissolved and the mixture has thickened.

4 POUR FORMULA INTO THE BOTTLES
Once the formula is prepared, use a sterilized plastic funnel to transfer the milk carefully into sterilized bottles.

5 SEAL AND STORE THE BOTTLES
Place the nipples in the bottles upside down, so they stay clean until ready for use. Cover with discs and screw on the rings. Put caps on the bottles and store immediately in the fridge.

BOTTLEFEEDING YOUR BABY

The two main benefits of bottlefeeding are that you can see how much milk your baby is taking in, and more importantly, that other family members can experience the special bonding feeding creates.

To recreate the intimacy breastfeeding permits, sit yourself comfortably in a chair or on the sofa with plenty of cushions for support. Keep distractions at bay; unplug the phone and have older children occupied in another room. Play some music to help you relax and enjoy the occasion. You may even like to bottlefeed topless so your baby can feel and smell your skin while he feeds.

Formula milk takes longer to digest than breast milk so you don't have to feed your baby as frequently as you would if you were breastfeeding. Babies should be fed on demand and most newborns will need feeding every two hours, although this can vary in accordance with your baby's particular needs. After about one month your baby may require feeding every three hours, and by two to three months of age he may only need feeding every four hours.

Use the smaller, 4-ounce bottles to feed a newborn baby and switch to 8-ounce bottles after about two months of age.

Always start feeding with a fresh bottle of milk each time and never refrigerate and reheat a previously warmed bottle.

YOUR OLDER BABY

As your baby matures, his sucking ability increases and he will be able to consume milk at a faster rate. You can help by making the size of the hole in latex rubber (but not silicone) nipples larger so the milk flows faster. Put the eye of a needle into a cork end, then sterilize the point by placing it over a flame. Slowly insert the point into the hole of the nipple to make it larger.

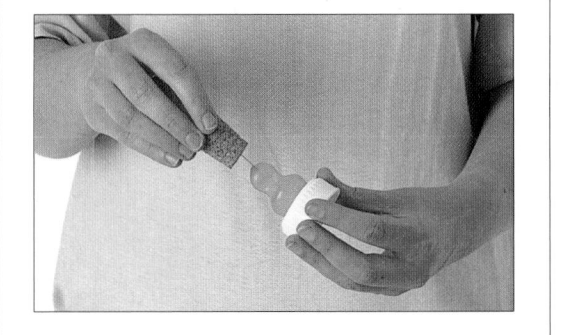

WARMING MILK

Most parents prefer to warm bottled milk to make it more closely resemble breast milk. Most babies, however, don't mind it being cooler as long as the milk is at room temperature, not cold. To warm up a bottle place it in a bowl of hot water and leave for a few minutes. Never use a microwave as this heats the milk unevenly and could burn your baby's mouth.

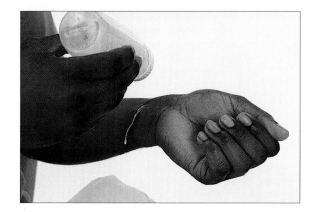

1 CHECK TEMPERATURE
Test the temperature of the milk before giving it to your baby by shaking a few drops onto your wrist. It should feel warm but not too hot.

2 LOOSEN THE TOP OF THE BOTTLE
As your baby sucks, negative pressure can make the nipple collapse. Loosening the ring slightly allows air to get in, replacing the milk that your baby has drunk, and keeps the nipple erect.

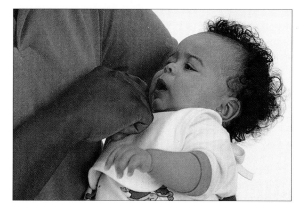

3 ELICIT THE ROOTING REFLEX
If you stroke his cheek, your baby will automatically turn his head toward you with his mouth open, ready to suck.

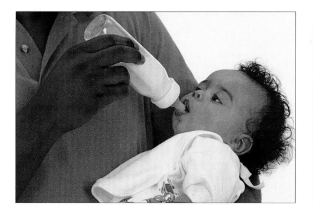

4 INSERT THE NIPPLE INTO YOUR BABY'S MOUTH
Angle the bottle at about 45 degrees so that the neck of the bottle is full of milk and there are no air bubbles. Place into your baby's mouth.

5 HELP YOUR BABY TO LATCH ON
Make sure the nipple is well placed in your baby's mouth and does not slip about, preventing proper sucking. Hold the bottle steady and adjust the angle as he drinks so that the top of the bottle is always full of milk.

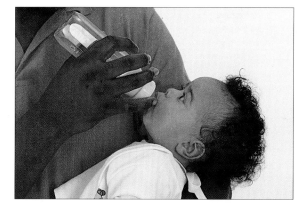

6 REMOVE THE BOTTLE
When your baby has finished the bottle and he hasn't let go, or you want to remove the bottle in order to burp him, slip your little finger into the side of his mouth to break the suction.

A SPECIAL TIME

Feeding is just as much about emotional nourishment as it is about meeting nutritional needs. Take this time to relax with your baby, to communicate your love and to establish a special rapport.

" We both took to the bottle right away! I enjoy giving it as much as my son likes being fed. "

BURPING YOUR BABY

Whether you breastfeed or bottlefeed your baby, he will take in air along with the milk he ingests. This air forms bubbles in his stomach and can cause discomfort as well as a feeling of fullness. If your baby's stomach hurts, he may cry (see Soothing a crying baby, pages 18-19). If he feels full, he probably won't continue feeding but very soon he will be hungry again. Therefore, you should try and get your baby to expel this accumulated air. Breastfed babies are able to make a tighter seal around their mothers' nipples than bottlefed babies around a bottle's nipple, so it is usually sufficient to burp a breastfed baby after he has finished each breast, while a bottlefed baby should be burped more often – after every few ounces. Don't interrupt a feeding to burp your baby, however; you should wait until your baby pauses naturally.

BIBS

While being burped, it is quite common for babies to spit up some milk. It is a good idea, therefore, to protect your baby's clothes with a bib, and your own clothes with a cloth or diaper. A plastic-backed bib provides the most protection.

• ON YOUR SHOULDER
Lift your baby up so that his head is over your shoulder and facing away from your neck. Use one hand to support his bottom and the other to gently rub or pat his back.

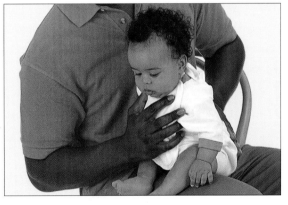

• SITTING UP
Gently raise your baby into a sitting position on your lap. Support his chest with one hand while you use the other hand to gently rub or pat around his shoulder blades.

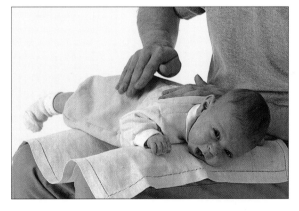

• ACROSS YOUR KNEES
Lay your baby down so that his tummy rests on one knee and his chest on the other. His head should face away from you and nothing should obstruct his mouth. Gently rub or pat his back with one or both hands.

BREASTFEEDING YOUR BABY

A mother's milk contains all the nutrients her baby needs to grow, and it helps to build up her baby's immune system during the crucial early months. It is also very convenient; a breastfeeding mother does not need to fuss with preparing formula or sterilizing bottles, and her milk comes virtually on demand at the right temperature. Also, the skin-to-skin contact a mother experiences with her child is unique and fosters mutual love and intimacy.

Your baby's growth during the first six months will be the greatest of her life. At about four months most babies will have doubled their birth weights and by a year they will have roughly tripled them. For physical growth and normal mental development to occur your baby needs to have a healthy diet and nurse regularly.

DEMAND FEEDING

Sometimes, mothers worry that their babies are not getting enough milk, or that their breasts are too small and their milk supply is inadequate. Milk is produced in the glands of the breasts and not in the fatty tissue, so breast size has no relation to a mother's ability to produce breast milk. As long as you take your cues from your baby and feed on demand, your baby should get the nourishment she needs. Regular weight checks at the doctor's will confirm this.

Feeding on demand depends entirely on your baby; some babies like to feel full all the time so may require feeding every hour. Others may nurse every four hours.

The amount of milk you produce is dependent on the amount your baby takes. Your breasts are stimulated by your baby to produce the milk she requires, so it is important that you are guided by her appetite and not restricted by a schedule.

BENEFITS OF BREASTFEEDING

Breastfed babies suffer less from gastro-enteritis, chest infections and measles, and because breast milk is more easily digestible than cow's milk, breastfed babies rarely become constipated. Breastfeeding mothers usually regain their shapes much more quickly than bottlefeeding mothers because oxytocin, the hormone that stimulates milk production, also makes your uterus contract, and this encourages your abdomen to return to its prebirth size. Breastfeeding also can reduce a woman's risk of breast cancer.

ALTERNATE BREASTS

Always offer your baby both breasts while nursing to ensure an adequate milk supply and to help prevent nipple soreness.

Nurse on one breast until your baby has emptied all the milk. Burp her, then offer the other breast. Your baby won't always need both breasts at every feeding, so alternate the breast you start with at the beginning of each session. This ensures that both breasts are emptied at least every other feeding. To help remind you which breast you started with the last time, attach a ribbon to your bra strap.

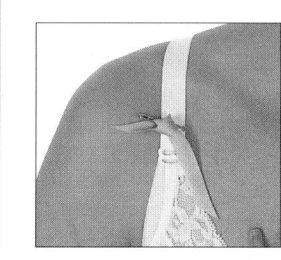

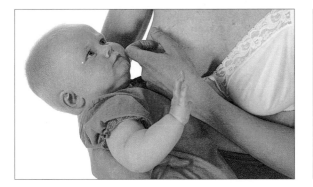

1 ENCOURAGE THE ROOTING REFLEX
Position your baby so that she is comfortably cradled in your arms. Stroke your baby's cheek so that she turns toward you, ready to suck.

4 ESTABLISH EYE CONTACT
Breastfeeding can be a relaxing and rewarding experience; talk, smile and look at your baby while she nurses. Let her play at the breast so she associates feeding with the pleasurable feel and smell of your skin.

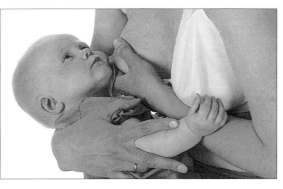

2 OFFER YOUR NIPPLE
Hold your breast with your free hand, bringing the nipple close to your baby's mouth. If she does not automatically open her mouth then use your nipple to tickle her lips and cheek until she does open it.

5 REMOVE YOUR BREAST
Once you feel your breast is drained of its milk supply, slip your little finger into the side of your baby's mouth to break her suction. Don't pull away before she has released your nipple as it can be very painful.

3 CHECK SHE LATCHES ON PROPERLY
To feed successfully, your baby's mouth should cover the whole of your areola, forming a tight seal. You should feel her tongue pressing your nipple against the palate of her mouth and see her jaws moving as she sucks.

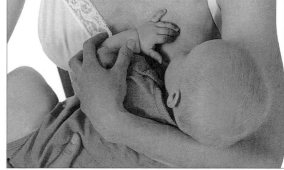

6 OFFER THE OTHER BREAST
Before you transfer your baby from one side to the other, burp her (see page 29). Cradle your baby comfortably in your other arm and offer her the second breast to suckle.

Breastfeeding positions

Although many mothers sit upright on a low chair or with their backs propped up against furniture while nursing, there are times when nursing in bed will be more comfortable or convenient. While your baby is young, experiment with different positions so your baby doesn't insist on latching on in only one. It is a good idea, too, to change positions throughout the day to prevent undue soreness in one part of the breast.

• Clutch hold

This is a useful position to try if your baby wriggles and arches her back when feeding or if you've had a Caesarean section. Sit upright with your feet close together and your knees up. Put a pillow on your lap and place your baby on her back with her face facing you. Support her head and neck with your hands and use your arm to hold her body close to your side.

• Reclining position

This is a useful position if you have had an episiotomy and find it painful to sit. It is also good for night feedings. Lay down on your side with plenty of pillows to prop you up and keep you comfortable. Place your baby in the crook of your arm with her mouth in line with your breast. Bring her close to you and offer your breast with your other hand.

EXPRESSING BREAST MILK

There may be times when you cannot be there to breastfeed your child but you would still like your baby to be given breast milk. To do so, you must express milk beforehand. Once you have collected enough milk – by hand or with a pump – in a sterile bowl, use a sterile plastic funnel to transfer small quantities of the milk into sterilized bottles. After sealing you should label the bottles with the date and time of expression. You can store expressed milk in the freezer for up to two months but you must freeze it right away. If it is stored in the refrigerator, use it within the next 24 hours.

You may also need to express milk if your breasts become engorged, that is, hard and full of milk. Expressing eases the pain and increases the milk flow.

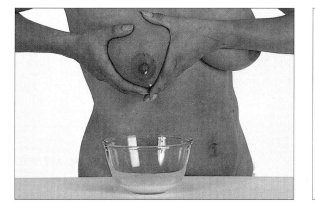

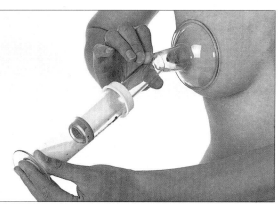

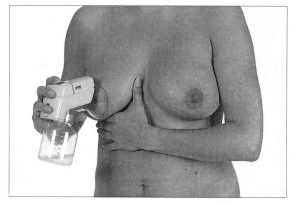

• HAND EXPRESSION
Skin-to-skin contact is the best way of stimulating your milk ducts. Make sure your hands are clean and massage your breasts well. Gently stroke down toward the areola and nipple then place your thumbs above the areola and your fingers below. Develop a rhythmic motion of squeezing then pressing back toward your breastbone. After a few minutes, your milk should appear.

• MANUAL PUMP EXPRESSION
A variety of hand pumps are available to make expressing milk faster. The syringe-style pump is the most effective. It has inner and outer cylinders and works by suction, drawing out milk in a piston-type action. Make a tight seal over your nipple with the funnel on the inner cylinder, then draw the outer cylinder in and out in a steady motion for a few minutes until your milk appears.

• MACHINE PUMP EXPRESSION
Battery operated machine pumps and small electric ones are available for home use. These pumps express milk quickly by performing the squeezing motion automatically. Machine pumps generally come with a fitting that enables milk to be expressed directly into feeding bottles – making them slightly more convenient to use.

FEEDING YOUR BABY SOLIDS

Introducing your baby to foods other than milk is a big step in your baby's development. Babies should not be given solids before three months of age, but after this there are no hard-and-fast rules. Seek your doctor's advice if in any doubt.

Generally, a change in your baby's feeding habits tells you when to start, and from there you should proceed gradually – he will show you what foods he likes and set his own pace.

A young baby can be fed in your lap or in an infant seat. Long-handled weaning spoons with plastic bowls can make feeding easier and safer. Be sure to sterilize the spoon and bowl before use and protect your baby's clothes with a bib. It may take up to a month on solids for your baby to master the technique of taking the food from the spoon.

apple sauce

yogurt and raspberry puree (after six months)

rice cereal

carrot puree

sweet potato puree

baked potato

PUREEING BABY FOOD

At this early stage, all foods must be smoothly pureed to a semi-liquid state – the texture of heavy cream. Use a blender with a sieve, or a 'mouli' which can both liquidize and sieve. Baby (gluten-free) cereals are often used as starter foods as they have plenty of calories and iron. Other candidates for first foods include potatoes, carrots, and apple sauce. Avoid eggs which may cause allergies.

• BEGINNING SOLIDS

At first you will simply want to introduce a couple of spoonfuls during bottle- or breastfeeding. Do not, however, cut down your baby's supply of milk. The pureed food provides only a few extra calories and your baby will still get his essential minerals, vitamins and protein from milk. Over the next few weeks, gradually increase the amount of solids you offer; your baby's need for nourishment from milk will reduce accordingly.

• GIVING A VARIETY OF FOODS

Try a wide mix of foods but introduce them slowly. Wait a few days after each new food to check for any negative reaction. Your baby will probably prefer blander foods to start with, so avoid spicy tastes.

• SPOONFEEDING

Protect your clothes with an apron or cloth. Hold your baby in an upright position in your lap. Scoop up some of the puree with a long-handled, non-brittle weaning spoon and put it just between her lips so that she can suck the food off. Put the spoon too far in and she may gag. A lot of the food may reappear until she gets the hang of cleaning off the spoon.

HELPING YOUR BABY FEED HIMSELF

At around six months of age a number of developments may change mealtimes significantly. Your baby's back and neck muscles may be sufficiently mature for him to sit in a high chair. Improved hand-mouth coordination may allow him to start using a cup. As his enthusiasm for food, ability to chew, and need to relieve gum irritation develop, he may start to feed himself – either gnawing on finger foods, or eating purees and porridges with a spoon.

But self-feeding also means more mess, so be prepared. Use a safe, stable, easy-to-clean high chair, and spread newspapers or a mat underneath to catch spills. Give your baby a small plastic spoon that won't break and has a limited flicking range, a molded plastic bib to catch the worst mess, and shatterproof plastic plates with suction cups on the bottom, which he can't turn over.

Success with self-feeding will not only give your baby confidence, but will allow him to join other family members at mealtimes, which will promote his sociability.

TRAINER CUPS

Unbreakable plastic feeding cups with weighted bases, tight-fitting lids with integral spouts, and double handles are recommended when weaning your baby off the bottle. He may prefer to start with water or fruit juice.

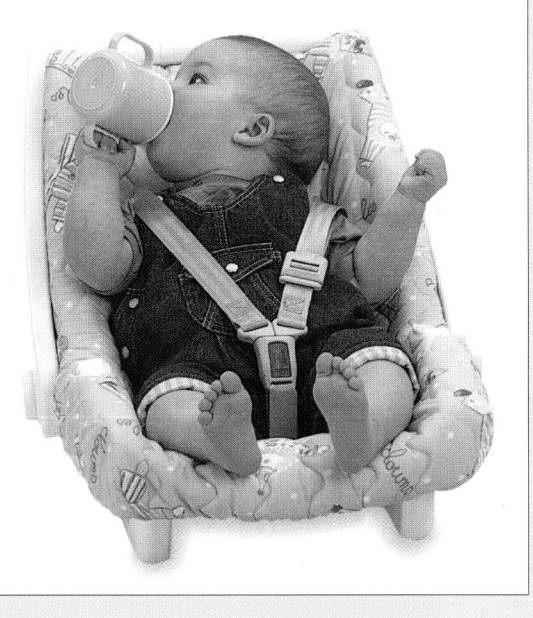

FINGER FOODS
Try easy-to-grasp sticks of carrot, cheese or apple; and small chunks of bread, toast, fish sticks, and bananas. Avoid giving nuts, fruit with seeds, unpeeled fruit that has a hard skin, and pieces of food that are too small. They may cause your baby to choke.

• OFFER FINGER FOODS

Firm chunks of food can be satisfactory to hold and gnaw on. Bananas are a popular choice – tasty enough to satisfy your baby's sweet tooth yet filled with essential vitamins and minerals. Always keep an eye on your baby while she eats to forestall possible choking.

• EATING WITH A SPOON

Once your baby's muscles are strong enough, sit her in a high chair but do not leave her unattended. Start off by offering her finger foods or feeding her yourself. She will most likely grab hold of the spoon and attempt to feed herself. A good tip is to load a spoon full of food and swap it for her empty one.

• EATING WITH HANDS

Don't discourage your baby's attempts to feed himself, even if he prefers to use his hands instead of utensils. Ignore any mess; it is important for him to practice feeding himself.

DIAPERS AND DIAPER CHANGING

Your newborn baby will urinate as much as 20 times a day in the first few months so you will spend a lot of your time changing his diaper. When you change your baby make sure you have everything you need by your side – fresh diaper, baby wipes, and a disposal sack in which to put the soiled diaper.

Being prepared means you don't have to leave your baby alone, wet and exposed. Never leave him unattended – even for a moment – on a raised surface; he could easily roll right off. Always clean your baby thoroughly at each changing (see pages 60-63) and make sure to wash your hands afterward.

PUTTING ON AND TAKING OFF A DISPOSABLE DIAPER

Disposable diapers are currently the most popular choice for parents because they are convenient, labor saving and easy to use. You don't have to wash or dry them, or worry about extra items such as pins, diaper liners or plastic pants. However, they are expensive to buy – particularly if you plan on having more children – and many people worry about their effect on the environment.

Disposables come in a range of sizes and you should make sure they fit snugly around your baby's thighs. The waist should be adjusted so that you can fit one finger between your baby's tummy and the diaper.

WATCH OUT!
A baby boy may be stimulated to urinate by the feel of air on his skin, so keep a spare diaper handy to cover his penis, if necessary.

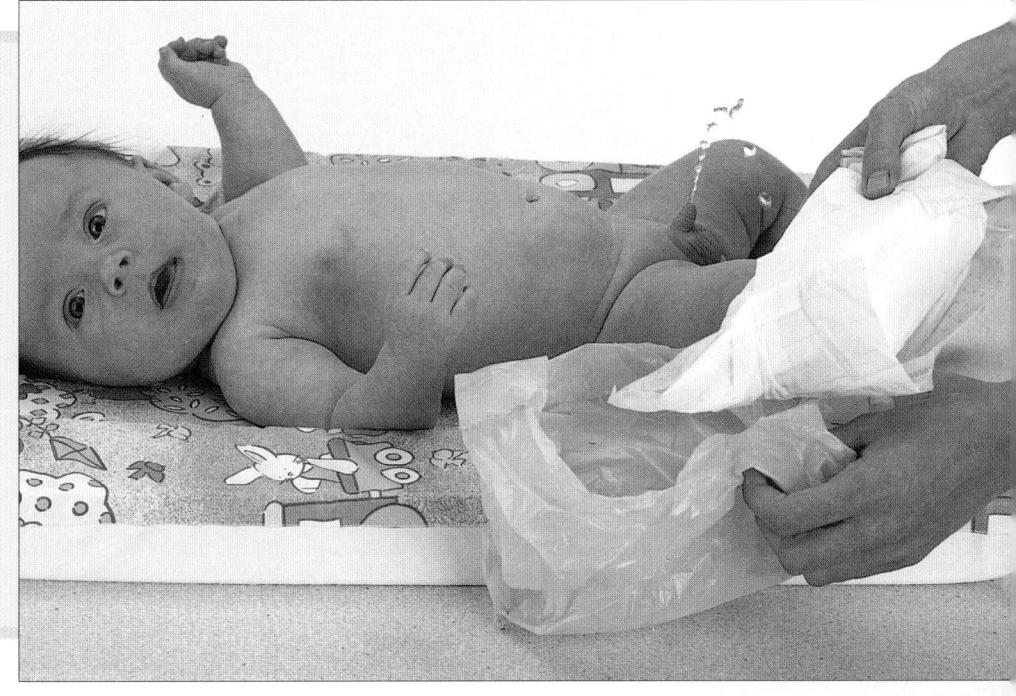

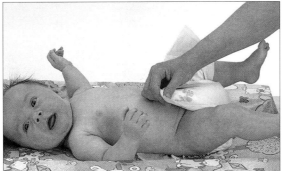

To put on a diaper

1 Open out the diaper and place under your baby's bottom

Lay your baby on his back on a changing mat or other flat surface. Lift his legs up by the ankles and slide an opened diaper under his bottom.

2 Bring the front up between your baby's legs

Gently let go of his ankles and bring the front of the diaper up between his legs. For a boy, make sure his penis points downward so he doesn't urinate into the waistband.

3 Fasten the sides

Smooth the diaper over his tummy. Bring one end into the middle, unpeel the protective backing to the tab and stick down. Repeat the process with the other end. Fold the top of the diaper in neatly against his tummy.

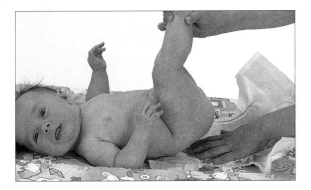

To take off a diaper

1 First unfasten the sides

Unpeel the tab from one side of the diaper, then the other. Take the front down between your baby's legs.

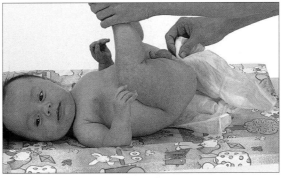

2 Use the diaper to clean any mess

Use the front of the diaper to wipe your baby's bottom clean of any excrement.

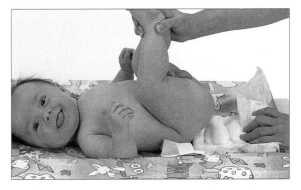

3 Roll up and remove

Fold the sides in toward the middle, roll the diaper up and slide it from under your baby's bottom. Retape the rolled-up bundle and dispose in a plastic bag or diaper sack.

PUTTING ON A FABRIC DIAPER

Fabric diapers can be folded in a variety of ways to suit the shape and size of your baby (see Other types of diaper fold, page 42). The most popular diaper fold for a young baby is the rectangle fold (see below). Self-stick shaped fabric diapers are also available (see page 43).

In certain circumstances, a properly folded fabric diaper will better contain urine and excrement than a disposable. A fabric diaper also allows more air to circulate around your baby's bottom so the chances of your baby's skin becoming irritated and developing diaper rash are reduced.

Fabric diapers are made of 100 percent cotton so are not waterproof by themselves; you will need to use some plastic pants on top. Terrycloth diapers are the most absorbent but also the most bulky. Flatter weave versions are also available. Fabric diapers along with plastic pants will make your baby's bottom a few sizes bigger, so keep this in mind when you are shopping for clothes for your baby.

Diaper liners, particularly 'one-way' types, which draw urine away from the skin, will help to keep your baby's skin drier and will prevent excrement soiling the diaper.

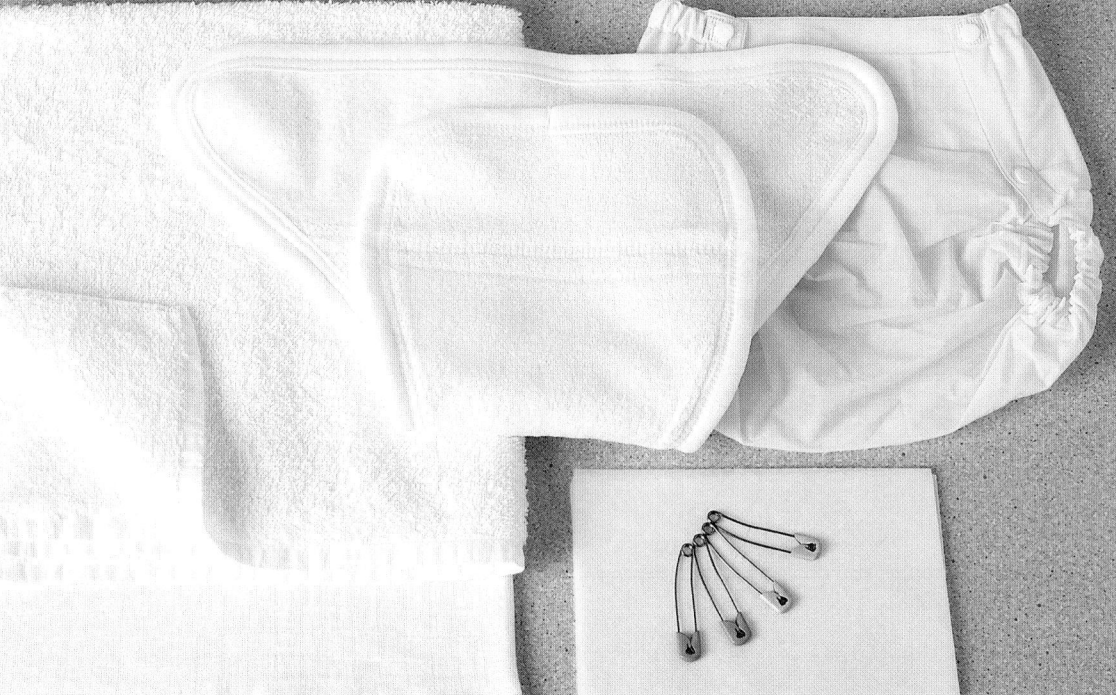

YOU WILL NEED

- fine muslin squares for a newborn
- standard square fabric or shaped fabric diapers for an older baby
- diaper liners (optional)
- diaper pins with safety heads
- plastic pants with snaps

1 PLACE YOUR BABY ON THE DIAPER

Fold the fabric square in half to form a rectangle. Fold the short side of the rectangle a third of the way into the middle. If you are putting a diaper on a girl, place the extra thickness under her bottom. For a boy, position the extra thickness at the front to give more protection over his penis. Lower your baby onto the diaper, aligning her waist with the top.

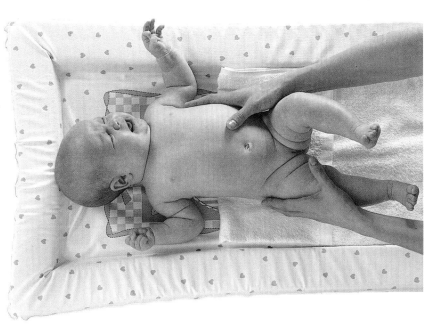

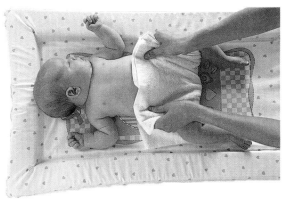

2 BRING THE FABRIC UP BETWEEN YOUR BABY'S LEGS

Gather the corners of the fabric in your hands and pull it up between her legs, smoothing the front over her stomach.

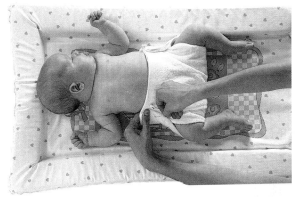

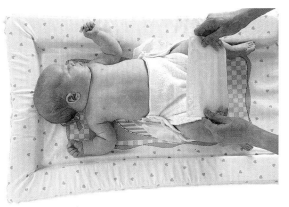

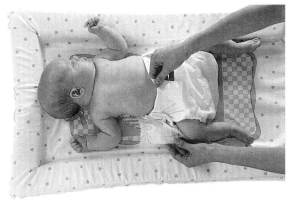

3 PIN THE SIDES

Keeping your hand between the fabric and your baby's skin, pin one side. Adjust the fit, then fasten another pin on the other side.

4 PUT ON THE PLASTIC PANTS

Holding her by the ankles, lift your baby's legs until her bottom is raised, then slide the opened plastic pants underneath her. Take the front of the pants up between her legs.

5 FASTEN THE SNAPS

Making sure the diaper is well tucked inside the plastic pants, fasten one side of the snaps, then the other.

OTHER TYPES OF DIAPER FOLD

The most popular fold for diapering is the rectangle fold (see Putting on a fabric diaper, pages 40-41), but there are a number of other ways to fold fabric diapers to suit your baby's particular shape and needs. The triangle fold is the simplest and requires one pin only. The kite fold produces a neater shape, is very absorbent and is suitable for a growing baby. You can adjust the size by varying the depth of the last fold (see box right).

TRIANGLE FOLD

On a changing mat or other surface, take two diagonally opposite corners of the square fabric and fold into a triangle. Place your baby on top of the diaper, making sure her waist is aligned with the top of the long edge of the triangle. Take one corner of the triangle into the middle, wrapping it well around your baby's tummy. Repeat with the other side.

Finish by taking the remaining point of the triangle up between your baby's legs and fasten all three layers with a large diaper pin.

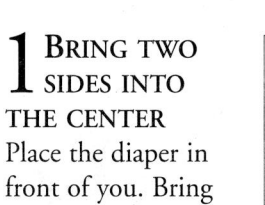

KITE FOLD

1 BRING TWO SIDES INTO THE CENTER
Place the diaper in front of you. Bring two adjoining sides into the center to produce a kite shape.

2 FOLD THE TOP POINT INTO THE CENTER
Take the point at the top of the kite and neatly fold it down into the middle.

3 FOLD THE BOTTOM POINT INTO THE CENTER
You can adjust the depth of this fold to make the surface area larger. Align the top with your baby's waist.

PUTTING ON A NO-PIN FABRIC DIAPER

Despite the fact that most parents choose to use disposable diapers, fabric diapers can work out to be cheaper in the long run, especially if you have more than one child. They also do less harm to the environment than disposable diapers.

Ready shaped fabric diapers with self-stick tabs, moreover, have many of the benefits of disposables, but can be used over a long period. They wash and wear like fabric diapers, but you don't need to spend time folding the cloth. Nor do you have to fiddle about with diaper pins or worry about accidentally pricking yourself or your baby.

No-pin fabric diapers have elasticized legs, which help protect against any leaks, but they are not as waterproof as disposables, so you have to use plastic pants on top (see Putting on a fabric diaper, pages 40-41). A diaper liner is also advisable.

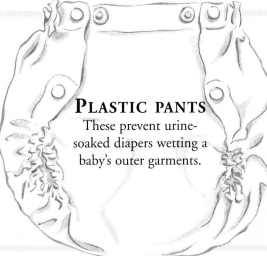

PLASTIC PANTS
These prevent urine-soaked diapers wetting a baby's outer garments.

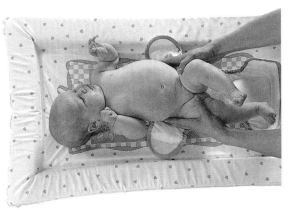

1 PLACE YOUR BABY ON TOP OF THE OPENED DIAPER
Open up the diaper and place on a changing mat. Put your baby on the diaper, aligning her waist with the top.

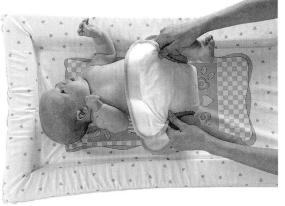

2 BRING THE FRONT OF THE DIAPER UP BETWEEN HER LEGS
Pull the front of the diaper taut and bring it up between your baby's legs. It should fit snugly, but not too tightly, around your baby's thighs.

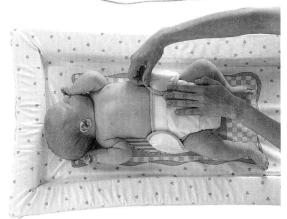

3 FASTEN THE SIDES
Bring one side over and fasten it to the self-stick tab on the waistband. Repeat on the other side. If the diaper is not fitting her tummy snugly enough, you can undo and refasten the sides.

TAKING OFF A FABRIC DIAPER

Most babies do not enjoy having their bundled-up bottoms exposed to the air, and may react negatively to having their diapers taken off, either by wriggling or crying. To make the process smoother, speedier and more enjoyable for both of you, have everything you need close by. This should include a clean diaper, wipes, fresh clothes and, if you are preparing to bathe your baby, a towel. You might like to have some special toys that your baby can play with, or a mobile in her line of vision which will entertain her while you change her.

To give your baby's bottom a chance to air and help prevent diaper rash (see Cleaning a girl, pages 64-65), incorporate play into your diaper-changing sessions. Use this time to tickle her, blow on and kiss her skin, and generally communicate with your baby. By doing this, you will make diaper changing more than just a mundane, smelly, but necessary task.

Bear in mind that a baby boy may be stimulated to urinate by the feel of air on his skin, so keep a spare diaper handy to cover his penis, if necessary.

" My baby really enjoys changing times. Perhaps she appreciates a clean bottom. "

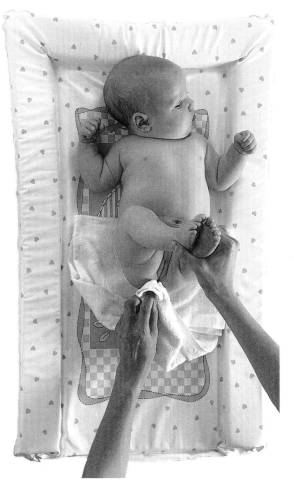

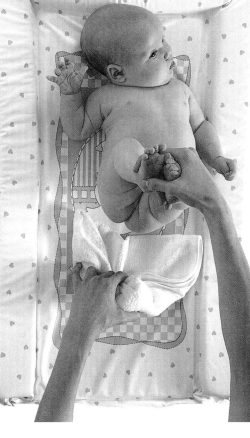

1 **UNFASTEN THE DIAPER**
Lay your baby on a changing mat. If using pins, place your hand between the fabric and her skin and carefully unfasten each one. Place pins out of your baby's reach. With self-stick diapers, simply pull back the fabric on each side.

2 **LOWER THE FRONT OF THE DIAPER BETWEEN YOUR BABY'S LEGS**
Slowly lower the diaper to check the damage. If there is any mess, hold your baby's ankles with one hand, raising her bottom, and use the edge of the fabric to wipe away any excrement.

3 **ROLL UP AND REMOVE THE DIAPER FROM UNDERNEATH**
With your baby's bottom still raised, fold the sides of the diaper into the middle and slide the diaper out from underneath her bottom, rolling it up as you remove it.

CARING FOR SOILED FABRIC DIAPERS

While re-usable fabric diapers have many advantages, washing, thoroughly disinfecting, and drying them is a laborious process. To minimize the fuss, make sure that you are well organized beforehand (see below). Incomplete cleaning can leave waste ammonia or bacteria on the diaper that can lead to diaper rash and infection. Using too much detergent on diapers, however, will irritate your baby's sensitive skin. Therefore, measure the amount of cleaner carefully and rinse everything twice.

To thoroughly sterilize diapers leave them to soak for at least six hours in a bucketful of sterilizing solution. Use different buckets for soiled and urine-soaked diapers.

With soiled diapers, scrape as much excrement into the toilet bowl as possible, then rinse them under the flush. If you are using diaper liners simply remove the liner with the stool and flush down the toilet. Then place the soiled diaper to soak in the bucket with the lid tightly sealed.

Rinse urine-soaked diapers under a faucet then wring out the moisture.

Wash plastic pants with some dishwashing detergent in water that is neither too hot nor too cold, otherwise they will go hard. If they do stiffen, soften them by tumble drying with some towels.

Alternatively, you can contract with a diaper service who will provide you with fresh supplies of diapers and a deodorized bin. They will collect soiled diapers on a regular basis. If you are prepared to meet the expense, their service can relieve you of a major chore.

YOU WILL NEED

- two different colored plastic buckets – one for soiled and one for urine-soaked diapers – with tightly fitting lids and strong handles; they should not be too big for you to carry when filled
- plastic tongs
- rubber gloves
- sterilizing solution

1 FILL TWO BUCKETS WITH STERILIZING SOLUTION

Always wear gloves when handling sterilizing solution and keep it out of the reach of older children.

3 USE TONGS TO REMOVE DIAPERS

Wring out diapers thoroughly and dispose of solution carefully. Rinse urine-soaked diapers in hot water and leave to dry. Wash soiled diapers on the hot cycle of your washing machine and rinse them twice.

2 PUT DIAPERS INTO BUCKETS

Rinse out urine-soaked diapers under a faucet then wring them out. Scrape off or flush excrement from soiled diapers into the toilet bowl. Submerge urine-soaked diapers in one bucket and soiled diapers in another. Leave to soak for at least six hours.

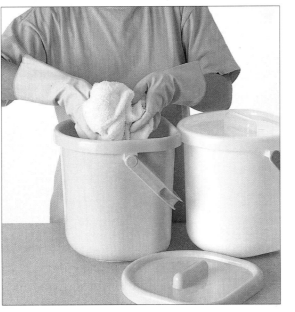

4 WASH PLASTIC PANTS

Add some dishwashing detergent to a bowl of warm water. Wash plastic pants in the bowl then take them out and leave to dry. If they become stiff you can soften them by tumble drying with some towels.

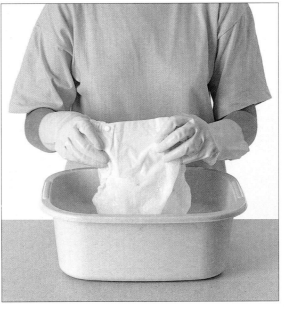

DRESSING YOUR BABY

Young babies generally don't like being dressed as they object to air on their skin and garments being placed over their heads. You can make it easy on your baby and yourself by having everything within reach and never leaving your baby alone on a raised surface – whether or not he can turn over.

Bear in mind that your baby's skin is very sensitive at this stage – make dressing fun with lots of nuzzling and kissing, but take extra care to be gentle. The clothes that you choose should reflect this sensitivity. Natural fabrics like cotton and wool will be warm and also allow your baby's skin to breathe, but avoid scratchy material – remember how much you hated itchy clothes when you were a kid!

"It's never too soon to be fashionable!"

PUTTING ON AN UNDERSHIRT

Your baby's ability to regulate his own body temperature is not fully functional for the first few months of his life. As a result, your baby can very easily get too hot or too cold. Unless it is very warm, always dress your baby in an undershirt. In very hot weather he may wear just an undershirt and diaper.

While undershirt designs vary (see page 50), they all account for the disproportionately large size of a baby's head. Their wide, loose necks allow easy access. This is particularly important for keeping your baby happy, since he will be easily upset by material dragging over his face.

When putting on or taking off an undershirt, make sure that you keep the fabric clear of your baby's face at all times. Using fabric softener in the wash will keep the shirt in the best condition.

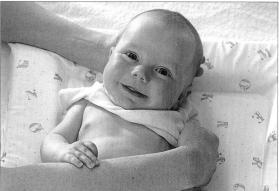

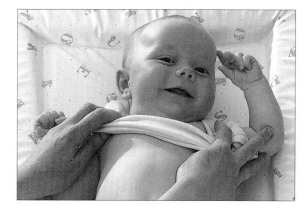

1 PLACE UNDERSHIRT BEHIND HIS HEAD
Using both hands, gather the material to the neck and stretch the opening as wide as possible. Place the shirt at the crown of your baby's head.

2 SLIP IT OVER YOUR BABY'S HEAD
Gently raise his head from the surface and, taking care not to scrape his nose or ears, stretch the shirt over your baby's face and neck.

3 ADJUST FABRIC AND LOCATE SLEEVE
Straighten the fabric around his neck. Take hold of one sleeve, gather up the material and insert your hand.

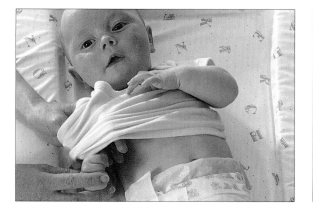

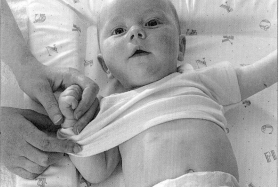

6 STRAIGHTEN THE UNDERSHIRT
Gently smooth the fabric down over his back and front and, if applicable, fasten the snaps between his legs. Take care not to pinch his skin.

4 REACH IN TO GRASP YOUR BABY'S HAND
Using your free hand, guide your baby's hand to the opening. Reach down to take hold of your baby's wrist.

5 PULL THE SLEEVE GENTLY OVER YOUR BABY'S ARM
Keeping hold of your baby's wrist, gently ease the sleeve over his arm with your free hand. Now put the other sleeve on.

DIFFERENT TYPES OF UNDERSHIRTS

Undergarments with wide neck openings will make it easier for you to dress your young baby and there are a variety of styles available. Snaps make a neat fastening but can be rough on a newborn's sensitive skin.

A good choice for a newborn baby is a crossover undershirt. This has ties at the side and can be put on like a cardigan (see page 57). Snap fastening versions are available. They are roomy enough so you can insert your hand between the snaps and your baby's skin and thus protect her sensitive skin. With this style your baby won't suffer the discomfort of having fabric pulled over her head and face.

As your baby grows you can use undershirts that have snaps along the shoulder ridge. These undo to make the undershirt neck opening much larger.

The most common device used by clothing manufacturers is the envelope neck. The material overlaps at the shoulder and, when you gather it up, stretches to make a wider neck opening.

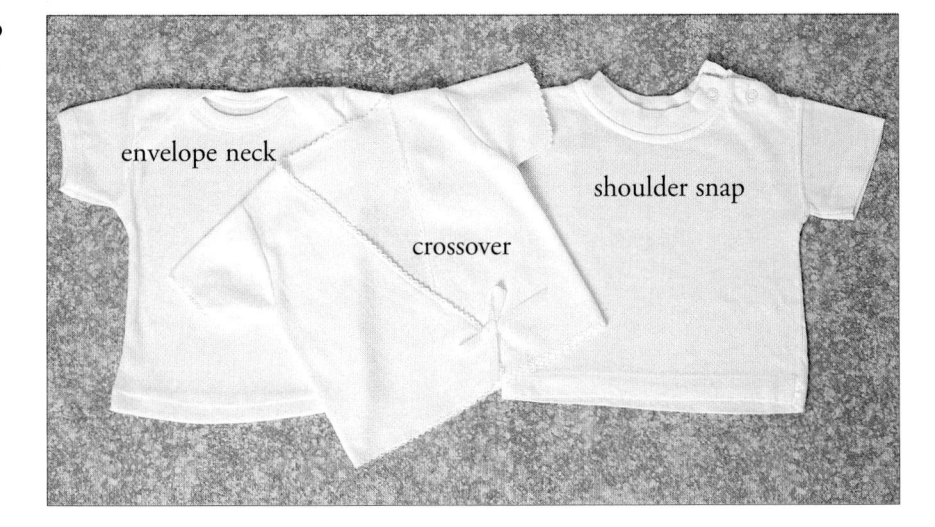

envelope neck

crossover

shoulder snap

ALL-IN-ONE STRETCH BODY

These are short-sleeved jumpsuits with snaps at the crotch. They don't ride up like bottomless undershirts and can keep your baby warmer. The envelope neck makes them easy to put over your baby's head, and the snaps allow you access when you want to change your baby's diaper. However, they are easily affected by leaking diapers so may need to be changed frequently.

TAKING OFF AN UNDERSHIRT

Babies get distressed by feeling cold air on their bare skins, and may get as upset having clothes taken off as they were about having them put on in the first place! So try to undress your baby somewhere warm, and be ready either to dress him again quickly, or to wrap him up in a warm towel or blanket.

As when putting an undershirt on, comfort your baby by nuzzling his tummy. Skin-to-skin contact is very important in promoting a loving relationship between a parent and his or her baby, and with dressing and undressing caregivers have excellent opportunities to foster this intimacy.

To take the undershirt off, begin by freeing your baby's arms. Slip the shirt over the front, then the back, of your baby's head. Make a game of bending down close and kissing his tummy as you lift off the shirt – he may never notice it's gone! As before, avoid dragging the material over your baby's face.

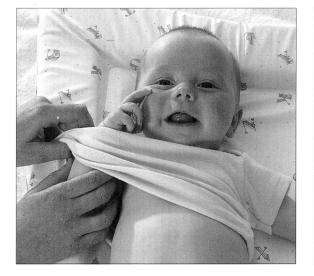

1 GENTLY EASE YOUR BABY'S ARM OUT
Gather the sleeve up in one hand and use your other hand to gently guide your baby's arm out of the sleeve. Repeat on the other side.

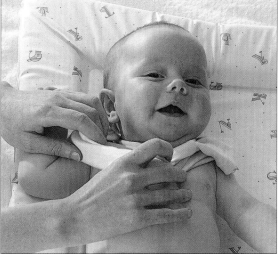

2 BRING THE SHIRT UP TO HIS NECK
Concertina the material at your baby's neck. Use both hands to stretch the opening of the neck as wide as possible.

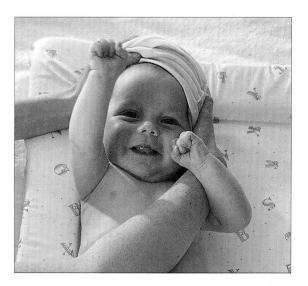

3 LIFT UP AND REMOVE THE SHIRT
Being careful to not touch his face with the material, pull the shirt up over his face to the crown of his head in one smooth motion. Then gently lift his head and take the shirt away.

PUTTING ON A JUMPSUIT

An all-in-one jumpsuit is a staple of most babies' wardrobes. It is easy to put on and take off, and covers the whole body, including the feet, so that you don't need to bother with booties.

When buying a jumpsuit, choose one that is colorfast and soft – natural fibers are usually better. When selecting the size, use your baby's height and weight as a guide, rather than age, since babies vary widely in their rates of growth. There is more bulk with a baby who wears fabric diapers.

If you have a choice, go for looser, baggier jumpsuits, which give your baby a bit of growing space. Pay particular attention to the neck, which should be wide and loose.

"At first it was like grappling with an octopus – arms and legs everywhere – but once I got the hang of the snaps, it became a two-minute job."

1 PUT THE FEET AND LEGS ON

Open out the jumpsuit on a non-slip surface and lay your baby on top of it. Gather up the material of one leg and slide it over his foot, making sure his toes go all the way in. Carry the material up his leg. Repeat for the other foot.

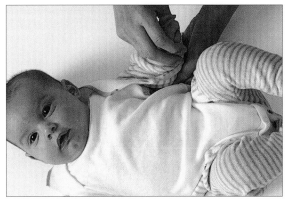

2 PUT ONE SLEEVE ON

Gather up the sleeve material and gently slide it over your baby's wrist, making certain that his fingers and nails don't get caught in the fabric.

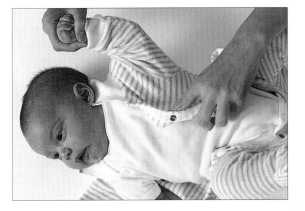

3 COVER HIS ARM AND SHOULDER

Slide the material down his arm and up over his shoulder. Pull on the material rather than his arm. If the sleeves are too long, fold back the cuffs so his hands are free. Now put on the other sleeve.

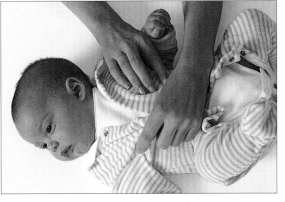

4 STRAIGHTEN THE TWO SIDES

Adjust the jumpsuit so the two sides meet in the center. Align the snaps.

5 FASTEN THE SNAPS

Starting at his crotch and working up to his neck, do up the snaps. It is easy to make a mistake at the beginning, so make certain you've joined the crotch snaps correctly.

TAKING OFF A JUMPSUIT

Your baby may need a change of clothes as frequently as a change of diaper. Jumpsuits make this chore a little simpler; they are easy to undo and take off, and you can leave your baby's chest covered while you attend to her bottom. This is particularly important as babies hate having their bare skins exposed to cold air. Having her skin bared may be why your baby kicks up a fuss at changing time – not because you are hurting her. As a precaution, make sure that the changing surface and room are warm, and have a towel or blanket ready to wrap her in.

You can try and make changing time fun, and an opportunity for closeness with your baby. By kissing, nuzzling and caressing her bare skin, you can bond with your baby and teach her about her own body.

Always be gentle when taking off your baby's clothes. Remember, the aim is to remove the jumpsuit from your baby, rather than your baby from the jumpsuit.

" When my mother watches me taking off my daughter's jumpsuit she always says how difficult I was to dress as a baby – all those frilly clothes! "

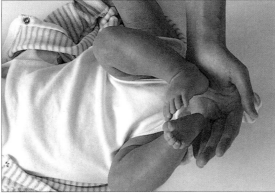

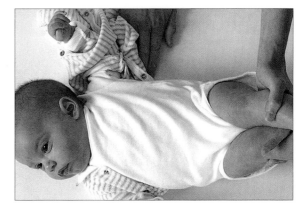

1 **REMOVE THE FABRIC FROM HER LEGS**
Undo all the snaps. Support her knee while you gently ease the material away from her leg. Repeat on the other side.

2 **CHECK TO SEE IF SHE'S WET**
Feel under her bottom to see if she needs changing. If you are only going to change her diaper, leave the suit on to keep her warm.

3 **SLIDE THE SUIT UP HER BACK**
If you're going to remove the suit, lift your baby's legs while you gently push it up under her back to her shoulders.

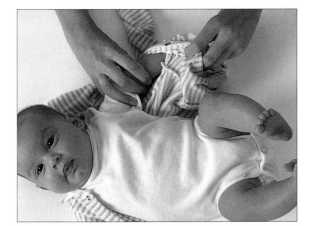

4 **REMOVE THE SLEEVES FROM HER ARMS**
Hold your baby's elbow while you gather up the sleeve and gently ease it away from her wrist. Repeat for the other arm.

5 **EASE AWAY THE JUMPSUIT**
Use your hand to support your baby's head and neck and raise her slightly. Gently draw the jumpsuit out from under her body.

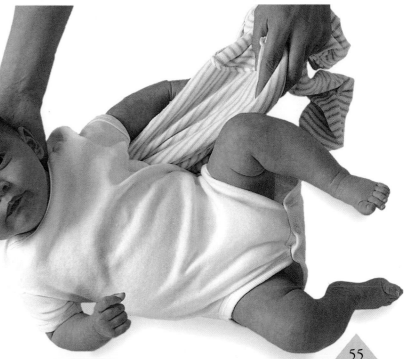

PREPARING FOR AN OUTING

It's never too soon to include your baby in your outings as long as you take certain precautions. It is a good idea to avoid crowds and rush hour transportation, where you may be jostled, and exposing your baby to people who may be ill.

There is no special age your baby needs to be before you can take her outdoors, as long as you are well prepared and your baby is well dressed. Your baby can't fully regulate her body temperature so always dress her in one more layer of clothing than what you would wear in the same environment.

A little preparation beforehand – in the form of a well-stocked travel bag – can help make outings highly enjoyable.

TRAVEL BAG ESSENTIALS

- changing mat with plastic backing – these sometimes come attached to the bag
- disposable diapers
- plastic bag or sack for diaper disposal
- cotton balls or diaper wipes
- baby lotion
- sunscreen lotion
- bottle of formula milk if you are not breastfeeding
- water or juice in a bottle
- some baby food and spoon
- bib
- muslin cloth to clean up any dribble
- rattle or other toy such as a soft book to amuse your baby
- pacifier (optional)
- change of clothes

KEEP HER HAT ON

A lot of heat is lost through an uncovered head so dress your infant in a hat. In warm weather a sunhat will help to protect her against sunburn.

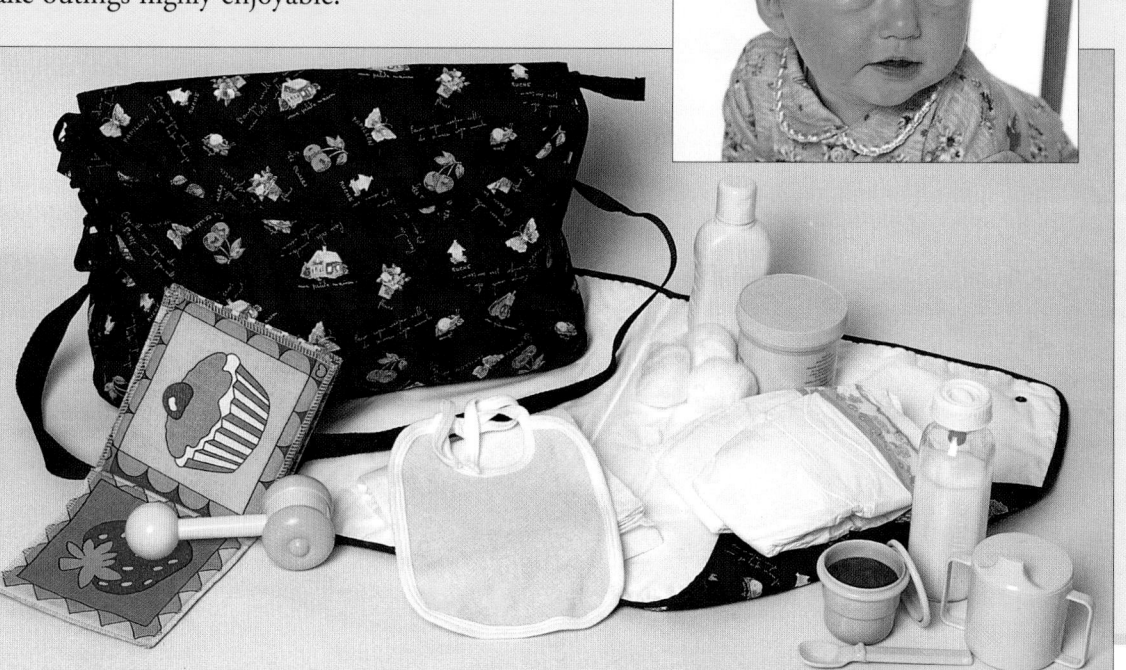

PUTTING A CARDIGAN ON YOUR BABY

There is a wide variety of outerwear to put on your baby once the weather turns cooler. For really cold weather, snowsuits with thermal linings are ideal and can be put on just as you would a jumpsuit (see pages 52-53). Otherwise, a cardigan and cap will suffice. Choose a flat textured sweater made of non-fuzzy fibers as this will prevent baby fingers from getting caught. Natural fibers such as wool will keep your baby warm without making her sweat. For milder weather a cotton cardigan is ideal.

1 PUT ONE SLEEVE ON
Sit your baby on your lap facing forward. Gather up one sleeve of the cardigan in your hands and take it over your baby's hand and wrist.

2 PUT THE SECOND SLEEVE ON
Gently ease the sleeve up over her shoulder, then bring the cardigan around her back. Gather up the other sleeve in your hands and prepare to place it over her other hand.

3 FASTEN THE BUTTONS
Pull the second sleeve up over her arm and, once the cardigan is fitting nicely, do up the buttons.

PUTTING YOUR BABY DOWN TO SLEEP

Provided that she is not too cold or hungry, your newborn baby may sleep for 60 percent of the time. Her readiness to sleep any time and any place can be a distinct advantage – until your baby has a regular night-time routine, you will be able to go out in the evenings and take your baby with you. It might, therefore, be advisable to buy something portable as a first bed – a carry cot, Moses basket or car seat with handles.

Your baby will sleep outside with no problem; just make sure that she is protected from drafts, mosquitoes and direct sunlight.

SIDS (SUDDEN INFANT DEATH SYNDROME)

SIDS (also known as crib death) is every parent's nightmare, causing the death of about 5000 babies a year. Thanks to a number of recent studies, a good deal is now known about how to avoid the risk factors that predispose children to become victims.

Most important is your baby's sleeping position. You should always put your baby down to sleep on her back or side. This factor alone resulted in a halving of the rate of crib death in Britain in the year it was first publicized. Another important risk factor is smoking – both during and after pregnancy. Exposure to one parent's smoke doubles the risk of a baby dying of SIDS.

SLEEP AIDS

As your baby gets older, she will start rolling over in her crib. Wedge-shaped sleep aids or rolled-up blankets can keep her on her back or side. Make sure, though, that her mouth and nose are not covered.

SIDS is more common in winter, probably as a result of babies becoming overheated or overwhelmed by heavy blankets. Use several light blankets instead of one heavy coverlet; they will give you finer control over your baby's temperature. Avoid insulators like crib bumpers, sheepskins and duvets.

YOUR OLDER BABY

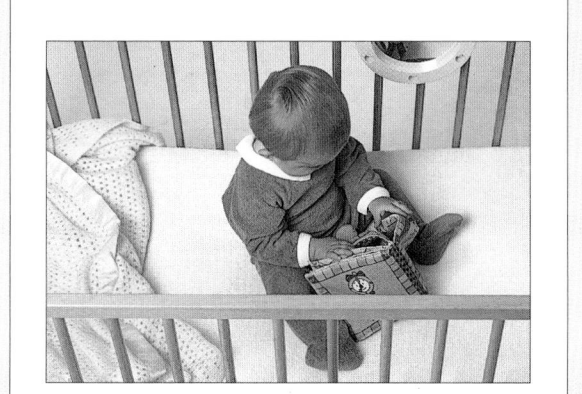

As your baby matures, you can avoid having to get up as soon as she does by putting some objects in the crib to amuse her. A soft fabric picture book or mirror will engage her attention. Avoid anything with sharp edges or strings.

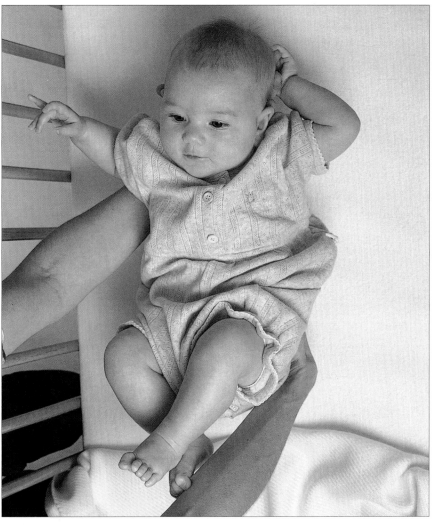

It is a good idea to put a baby monitor in your baby's crib. This will immediately alert you to your baby's cries.

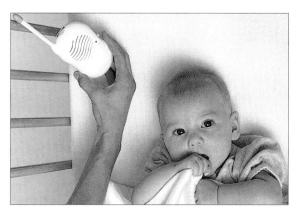

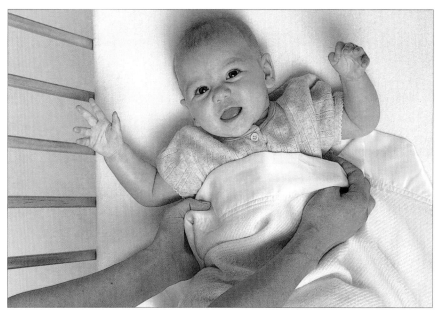

1 PLACE YOUR BABY ON HER BACK TO SLEEP

Always put your baby into her crib or carriage on her back or side. Research into SIDS has shown that this is the most effective way of reducing your baby's risk, although the precise mechanism is still unknown.

2 COVER HER WITH LIGHT BLANKETS

A sheet and a variable number of light blankets should be used. If possible, your baby should sleep on a new foam mattress with airholes, which is protected by a plastic sheet and topped with a cotton sheet.

KEEPING YOUR BABY CLEAN

Most babies love their bathtimes but not all of them do so right away. A newborn has extremely sensitive skin and a limited potential for getting dirty, so she will only need wiping down with water and cotton balls. Some doctors feel that babies should not be immersed in water until their umbilical cord stumps have fallen off and any circumcisions have healed.

Once you feel confident about giving your baby a bath, invest in a plastic baby tub and use only mild soaps and cleansers. Once your baby can sit up by herself, you can move on to a proper bath. By this stage, your baby will probably be looking forward to bathtime as one of the highlights of her day.

At first, though, your baby will probably object to being wetted and wiped, and in particular to feeling cold air on her bare skin. You can, therefore, delay a full bath until she is ready for one. When you do bathe her, do so as quickly as possible, and have a big, soft, fluffy towel warmed on a radiator. The key is to be prepared – have everything you need at hand and never leave your baby unattended in the bath.

CLEANING A NEWBORN

A simple once-over is all your young baby needs, since only her exposed areas – face, neck creases, hands, feet – and genitals and bottom are likely to become dirty. (See page 76 for advice on cleaning the umbilical cord area.)

To clean your newborn use cotton balls – a clean one for every pass – and cooled-down boiled water. Do not use tap water at this stage as you will be cleaning your baby's eyes, or talcum powder or soap as they will dry her very sensitive skin. Equally, avoid cleaning inside your baby's nose or ears; your baby's inner surfaces are lined with mucous membranes that clean themselves – interfering with them will do more harm than good. Your newborn's limbs may still be tightly curled up against her body, so you may need to gently pry them apart.

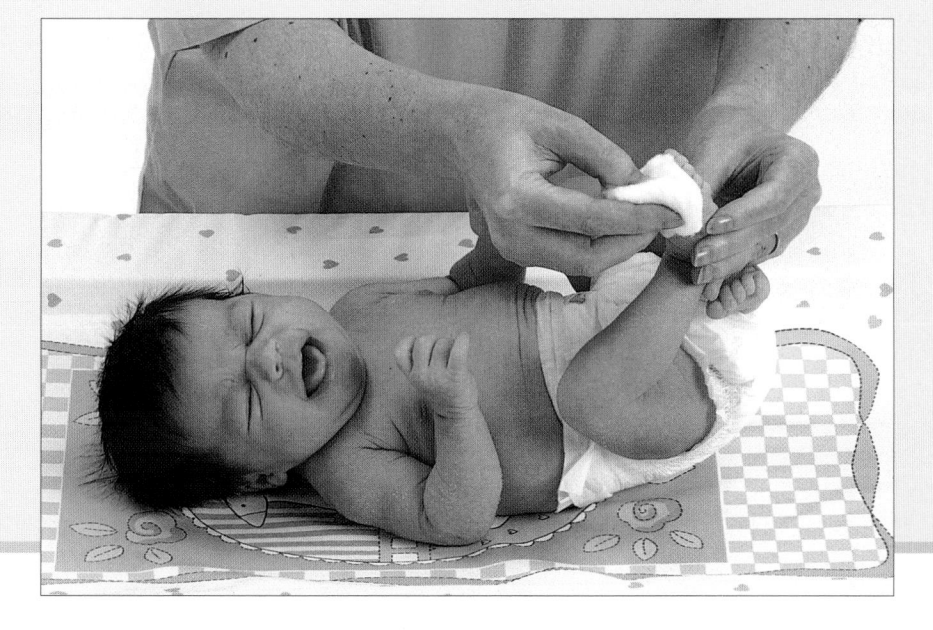

1 CLEAN AROUND HER EYES

Wet a cotton ball with the sterile water and wipe from the inner to the outer corner of her eye. Use a separate cotton ball for the other eye to prevent transferring infections. Wipe around and behind the ears, but not inside.

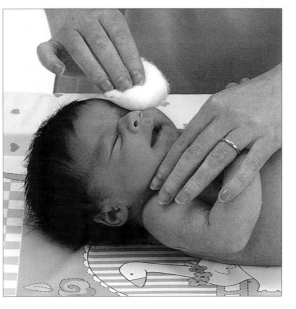

2 WIPE INTO HER NECK AND ARMPIT CREASES

With a fresh cotton ball, wipe clean her neck creases to get rid of any dried sweat or dirt that might cause soreness or irritation. Then gently lift each arm and wipe the armpit area, where the folds of skin can rub together and become sore. Thoroughly pat dry with a soft towel.

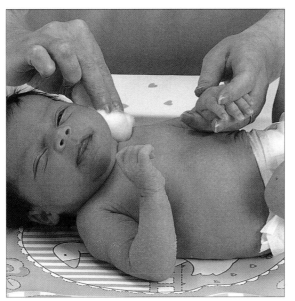

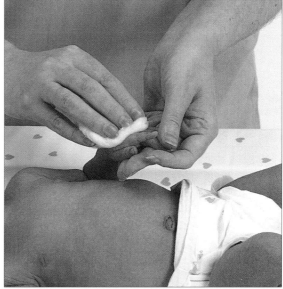

3 OPEN OUT HER HANDS

Use another cotton ball to wipe her hands, unclenching them to check for sharp fingernails and dirt between the fingers. Pat dry with a soft towel or cloth.

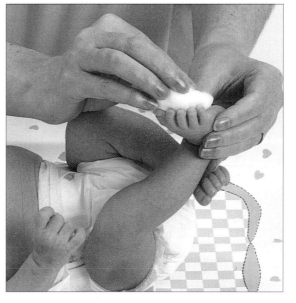

4 ATTEND TO HER FEET

Wipe the top and bottom of your baby's feet, and between her toes. They may be tightly curled so gently pry them apart. Again, pat dry with a towel.

CLEANING A BOY

Every time you change your baby boy's diaper you should clean his genitals and bottom. As his urine can spray widely, make sure you wipe down his abdomen and legs or the urine may remain on his skin and cause an irritation there.

CIRCUMCISION

A baby boy is born with skin that covers the end of his penis. Some parents choose to have this foreskin surgically removed – either in the hospital or at home in a religious ceremony. Known as circumcision, it leaves the tip of the penis exposed. The reasons for circumcision are deeply steeped in religious, social, cultural and esthetic traditions.

A circumcised penis is thought to be more hygienic, but the operation itself, although minor, can result in infection. Consult your pediatrician if you are undecided about whether to circumcise your baby boy.

If your baby is circumcised, watch carefully for any signs of infection. The operation will usually cause some swelling or bleeding. The circumcised penis will probably be covered in gauze which needs replacing every time you change your baby's diaper. Avoid getting your baby's circumcised penis wet until healing is completed.

When cleaning an uncircumcised baby never pull back the foreskin as it is very tight and could easily get damaged. It is sufficient to just clean the surface creases. After a few years, the foreskin will become loose and can be pulled back for cleaning. In the meantime, it will clean itself.

YOU WILL NEED

- bowl of cooled-down boiled water – once your baby is older you can simply use warm water from the tap
- plenty of cotton balls
- plastic bag for disposing of dirty cotton balls and soiled diaper
- clean diaper
- washcloth for any accidental spillages

REMOVE YOUR BABY'S DIAPER SLOWLY
When he feels the air on his skin your baby may urinate. To avoid getting sprayed, pull the front of his diaper back gradually.

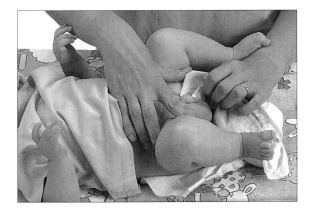

1 CHECK TO SEE IF HE'S DIRTY
Carefully pull back your baby's diaper and if he has made a mess, use the corner of the diaper to clean most of it up.

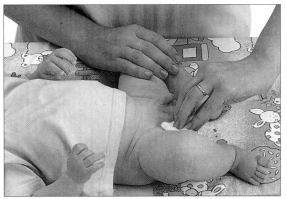

2 CLEAN BETWEEN THE CREASES OF YOUR BABY'S LEGS
Separate your baby's legs and, using a moist cotton ball, wipe well the folds of skin between his tummy and leg.

3 WIPE HIS PENIS CLEAN
Using fresh cotton balls, clean your baby's penis. Wipe downward, away from his body. Make sure you clean around his testicles as well.

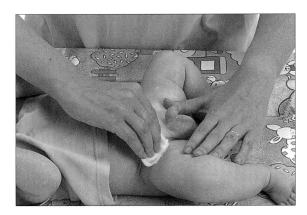

4 WIPE YOUR BABY'S UPPER THIGHS
There may be traces of urine on the upper part of his legs so wipe this area thoroughly, using another damp cotton ball.

5 CLEAN HIS BUTTOCKS
Hold your baby's ankles with one hand. Gently lift him so that his bottom is raised from the surface. Using clean moist cotton balls, wipe the backs of his thighs and his anal area. You may need to use quite a few cotton balls to do a thorough job of cleaning if he has had a bowel movement.

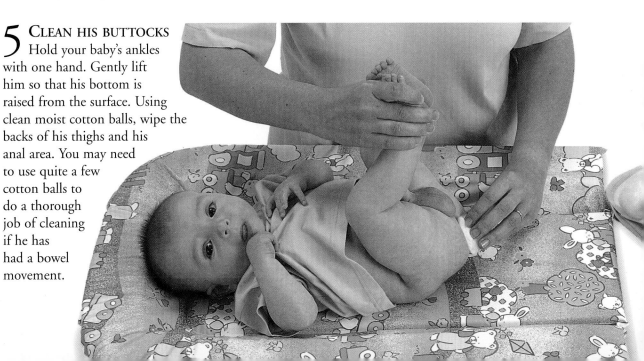

CLEANING A GIRL

When you change your baby girl's diaper, clean her bottom thoroughly. It is also a good idea to expose this area for a bit to give her skin a rest from being covered.

Don't try to clean inside your baby girl's vulva. This area is not likely to contain a lot of dirt and if you open up the folds you may introduce unnecessary infection. Always wipe from front to back so as not to spread any bacteria from the anus to the vagina, and use a fresh cotton ball for each swipe.

You may also notice some bleeding or a white discharge coming from your newborn's vagina. Usually this is due to maternal hormones still circulating inside her body. It is quite normal and should cease after a few days.

BOWEL MOVEMENTS AND MECONIUM

The first stools your newborn produces will be dark in color and sticky in texture. This is meconium – the substance which lined your baby's intestines while she was in the uterus. After meconium is passed her movements will become paler and firmer.

DIAPER RASH

Lost contact with sun and air, and frequent exposure to excess moisture and the chemicals contained in urine and feces, can irritate the skin and encourage infection. This can develop into diaper rash.

SIGNS OF DIAPER RASH
A red rash, or raised spots around the bottom or in the fatty folds between your baby's legs are sure signs.

BARRIER CREAMS
Generously spread some thick cream containing zinc oxide around the affected area during diaper changes.

AIR IS BENEFICIAL
To help expose your baby's bottom to air and sunshine, let her go without a diaper for short periods frequently throughout the day. Just after a diaper change is a good time.

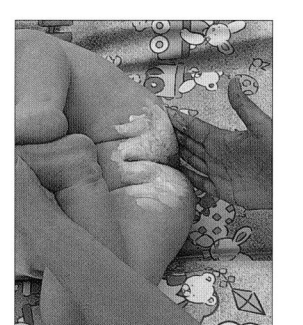

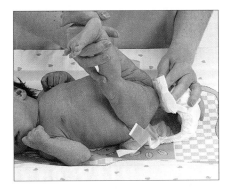
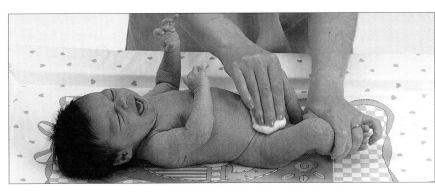

1 USE THE DIAPER TO CLEAN YOUR BABY'S BOTTOM
If your baby has had a bowel movement, use the edge of the diaper to clean some of the mess from her bottom.

2 CLEAN YOUR BABY'S TUMMY
Hold your baby firmly but gently on the changing mat. You may need to gently pry away the tightly curled limbs of a newborn from her torso. Moisten clean cotton balls in some cooled-down boiled water and use to wipe all over her tummy area. After the umbilical cord area has healed, you can use plain water.

3 WIPE INTO HER LEG CREASES
Taking a fresh cotton ball, clean into the folds of your baby's legs. Wipe firmly downward and away from her body.

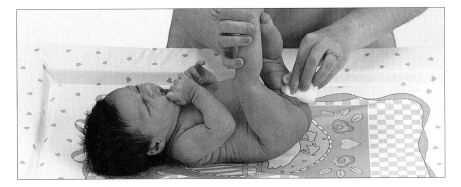
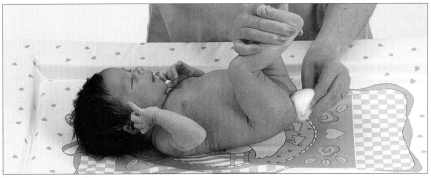

4 CLEAN YOUR BABY'S VULVA
Hold your baby's ankles with one hand and gently lift so that her vulva is exposed. Use fresh moist cotton balls to clean the outer lips of your baby's genital area. Do not open out the lips to clean inside. Use a fresh cotton ball for each swipe and always wipe downward, so that you don't transfer any bacteria from the anus to the vagina.

5 CLEAN HER BUTTOCKS
Still keeping your baby's bottom raised from the changing mat, take fresh moistened cotton balls and wipe her anal area clean. Make sure you also clean the backs of her thighs and up her back, if necessary.

GIVING YOUR BABY A SPONGE BATH

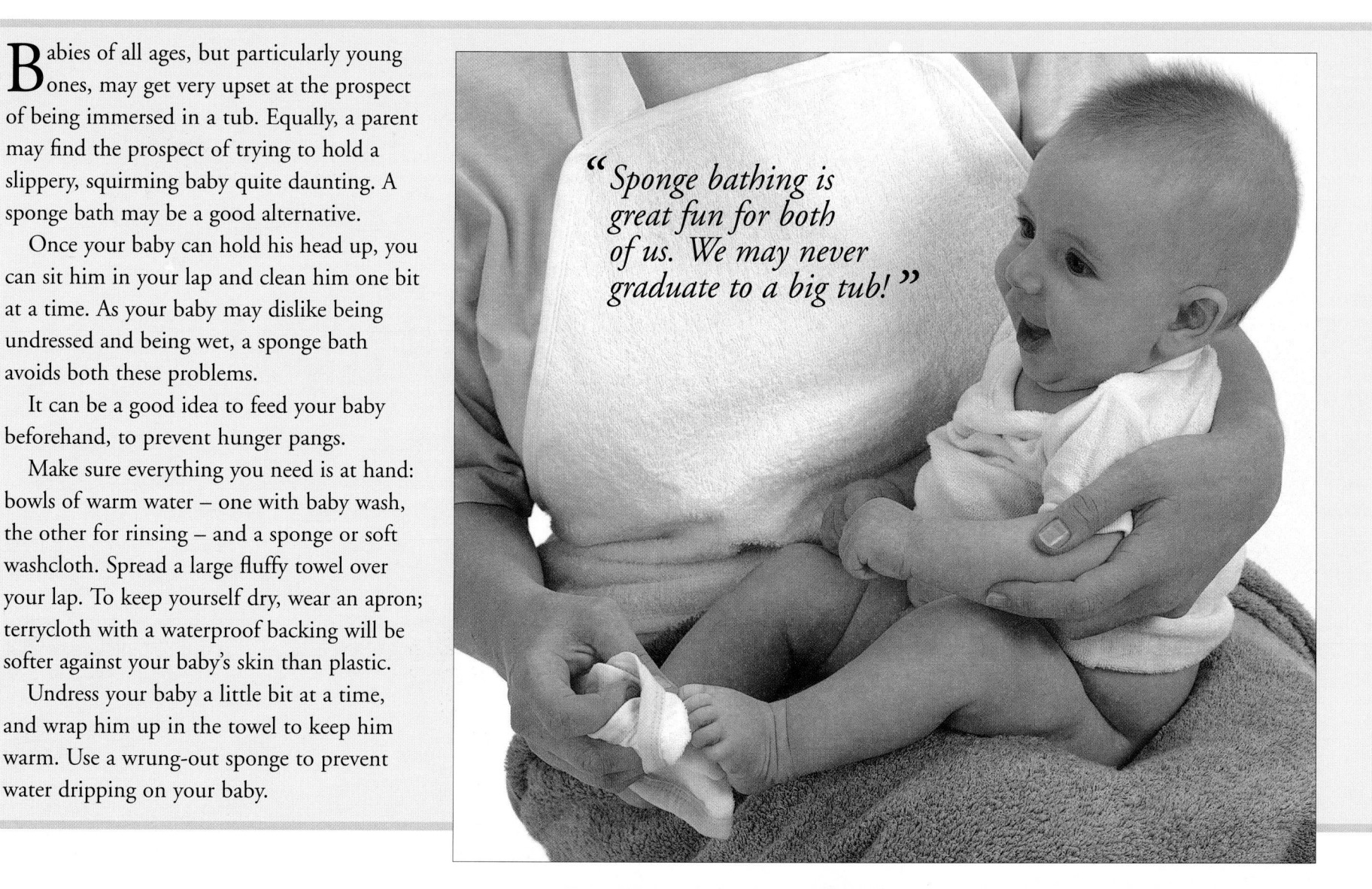

"*Sponge bathing is great fun for both of us. We may never graduate to a big tub!***"**

Babies of all ages, but particularly young ones, may get very upset at the prospect of being immersed in a tub. Equally, a parent may find the prospect of trying to hold a slippery, squirming baby quite daunting. A sponge bath may be a good alternative.

Once your baby can hold his head up, you can sit him in your lap and clean him one bit at a time. As your baby may dislike being undressed and being wet, a sponge bath avoids both these problems.

It can be a good idea to feed your baby beforehand, to prevent hunger pangs.

Make sure everything you need is at hand: bowls of warm water – one with baby wash, the other for rinsing – and a sponge or soft washcloth. Spread a large fluffy towel over your lap. To keep yourself dry, wear an apron; terrycloth with a waterproof backing will be softer against your baby's skin than plastic.

Undress your baby a little bit at a time, and wrap him up in the towel to keep him warm. Use a wrung-out sponge to prevent water dripping on your baby.

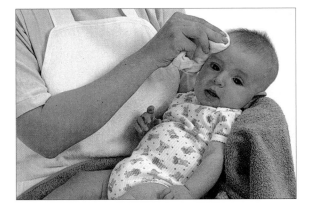

1 WIPE YOUR BABY'S FACE

Before undressing your baby, wet the cloth with clean water and wipe your baby's face, paying particular attention to the eye and mouth areas. Pat dry, if necessary.

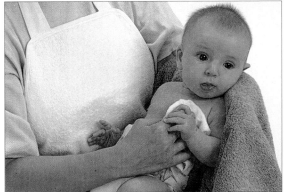

2 WASH HIS CHEST NEXT

Take off your baby's top. Wet the cloth with soapy water and clean his chest, making sure to wipe his skin folds and under the arms. Do not scrub. Rinse off the soap with clean water.

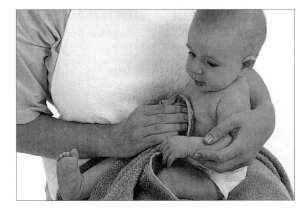

3 PAT HIS CHEST DRY WITH THE TOWEL

Pick up the end of the towel and use it to remove any water by pressing lightly.

4 THEN WASH HIS BACK

Supporting him with your arm, make your baby lean forward, then wash, rinse and dry his back. Put his top back on.

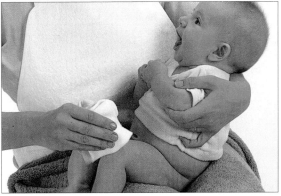

5 NOW ATTEND TO HIS LEGS

Remove his diaper, and with the damp soapy cloth, clean your baby's legs, paying particular attention to his thigh creases and the skin behind the knees. Rinse and pat dry.

6 FINALLY, WASH HIS FEET

Clean the top and bottom of his feet, and between the toes. Then pat dry.

WASHING YOUR BABY'S HAIR

In the first few weeks wash your baby's hair and scalp with warm water every few days to get rid of any built-up sweat and dirt. In the first few days you don't need shampoo, but once your baby has enough hair, use a mild shampoo. Comb or brush as necessary.

Your baby's attitude to having his head wet may well be at odds with this schedule. Babies especially dislike getting water on their face, so take care to avoid this. If your baby really hates having his hair washed, do not force him. Try simply wiping his head clean for a couple of weeks, and then try again.

HAIR SHIELD

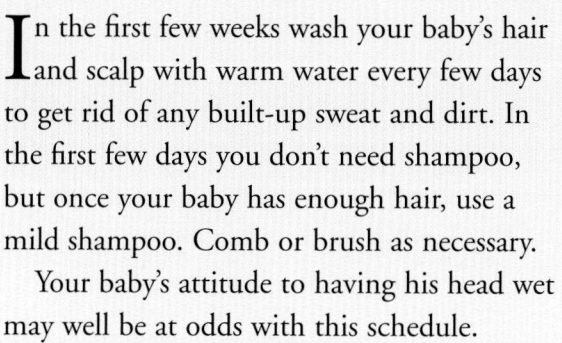

To prevent any shampoo or soapy water getting in your baby's eyes, you could try a cap like this, which fits around the hairline and catches any drips.

Bear in mind that your baby will not be happy unless he feels secure – if he objects to being held in the 'football carry' (see below), sit on the edge of the bath and hold him on your lap. Always use non-sting shampoo, but avoid getting it in the eyes anyway.

A common condition on the scalp is cradle cap (see Taking care of your baby's hair and nails, pages 78-79). It is no cause for concern and usually clears up after a few weeks.

THE FONTANELS

When your baby is born, the bones of his skull will not be entirely fused together, leaving small soft patches on the top of his head. These are known as the fontanels. While you should obviously be careful of these, since they are spots where your baby's brain is vulnerable, they are covered with a tough membrane, so you don't have to avoid them altogether. Simply wash and dry over them gently as you would the rest of your baby's skin. They won't knit together entirely until he is about two years old.

USING A SPONGE

If you worry about washing your baby's hair, or if he resists proper shampooing, you don't have to undress him or put him in a bath. Simply sit him on your lap as for a sponge bath (see Giving your baby a sponge bath, pages 66-67), and wash his head with a damp sponge or washcloth. Pat dry with a soft towel and gently brush.

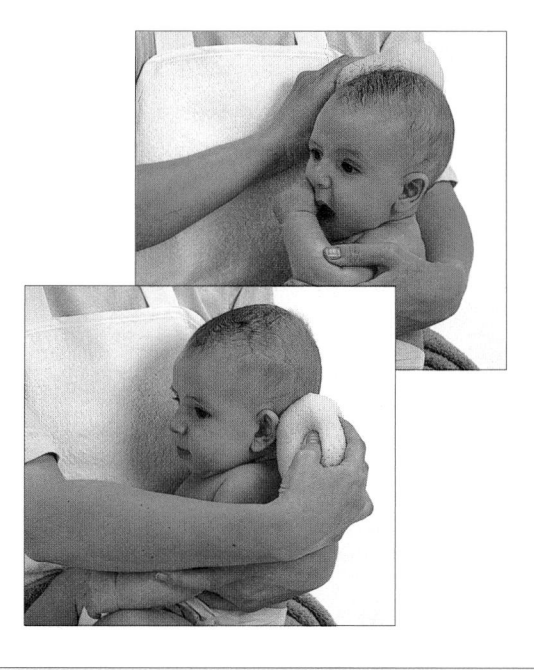

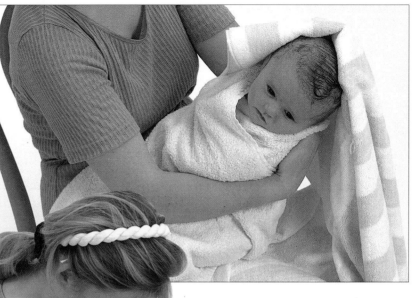

1 HOLD YOUR BABY IN THE FOOTBALL CARRY

Undress your baby and wrap her in a towel. Put her legs between your arm and side so you can grip them under your armpit. Support her back with the length of your arm and cradle her head with your hand. Bring her over to the basin or tub.

2 WET HER HAIR

Check that the water is not too hot with your elbow (see page 70). Use your free hand to take some of the water over her head onto her hair. Gently apply some non-sting baby shampoo onto her scalp, then rinse it off. If you like, you can add the shampoo to the bath water.

3 DRY YOUR BABY'S HAIR WITH A TOWEL

Gently pat, rather than rub, your baby's hair dry with another towel. Your baby may panic and cry if you cover her face with the towel, so use the corner. Gently brush her hair using a soft-bristled baby brush.

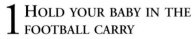

PREPARING TO BATHE YOUR BABY

Before you start bathing your baby, have everything you need at hand. The first rule of bathing is 'never leave your baby unattended in the tub.' By being well prepared you won't have to go looking for things holding a wet baby.

While you are using a portable tub to bathe your baby you can wash her in any room. Make sure the room is sufficiently warm, and the tub is well supported on a waterproof surface away from any drafts.

YOU WILL NEED

- bath tub with a textured non-slip base
- waterproof apron with plastic backing
- mild baby toiletries
- small bowl of cooled-down boiled water
- cotton balls
- large, soft towels
- sponge or soft washcloth
- clean diaper and clothes

TEST THE WATER

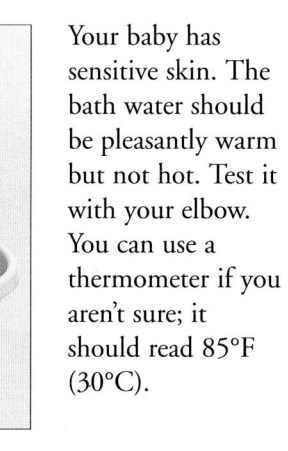

Your baby has sensitive skin. The bath water should be pleasantly warm but not hot. Test it with your elbow. You can use a thermometer if you aren't sure; it should read 85°F (30°C).

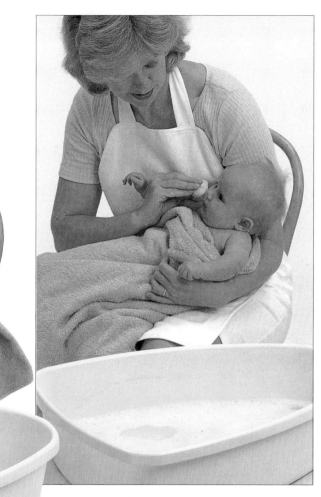

1 PARTIALLY UNDRESS YOUR BABY
Remove your baby's diaper and all her clothes down to her undershirt. Sit down near the tub, cover your lap with a towel and prepare to completely undress her. You can put a spare diaper under her bottom to protect your clothes in case she urinates.

2 REMOVE HER CLOTHES COMPLETELY
Gently stretch the neck of the undershirt over your baby's face to remove. Wrap the towel around her to keep her warm.

3 CLEAN YOUR BABY'S FACE
Using clean cotton balls and cooled-down boiled water for a young baby, clean around her eyes and mouth. For an older baby you can use a washcloth and plain water. If you want to shampoo your baby's hair (see pages 68-69) do it now before putting her into the tub.

BATHING IN A TUB

Until your baby can sit up unsupported – at about seven months of age – bathe her in a small plastic tub set at about waist height to avoid hurting your back. If you are buying a bath stand, make sure that it is very stable. Putting a rubber mat in the bottom of the bath will make it less slippery and give your baby more grip, but you should support her back and shoulders with one hand the entire time you are holding her. Above all, never leave your baby unattended.

Help your baby enjoy her bath by smiling and talking to her throughout; be gentle and avoid getting water on her face. Take care to ensure that the bath water remains warm.

Some parents prefer to soap their baby before putting her in the bath. Others put liquid baby soap in the bath water. In general, wash the cleanest parts of your baby first and the dirtiest parts last. This way you cut down on the risk of transferring germs from one part of her body to another.

BATH AID

A rubber mat in the bottom of the bath will make it less slippery and thus more secure. You can also purchase foam supports that hold your baby in a safe position.

" She should have been stamped, 'slippery when wet!' "

1 LOWER YOUR BABY INTO THE TUB

Unwrap your baby and cradle her in your arms, supporting her bottom half with one hand and her shoulders and head with the other. Lower her slowly into the tub, bottom first.

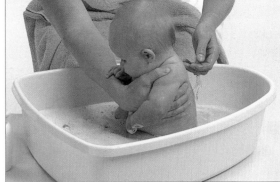

2 RINSE HER TORSO

Support your baby in an upright position while you gently splash water onto her chest and stomach. Smile and laugh to amuse her.

3 WASH HER UPPER BACK AND NECK

Sit your baby up, holding her under the armpit and supporting her chest across your arm. Rinse her upper back and the back of her neck.

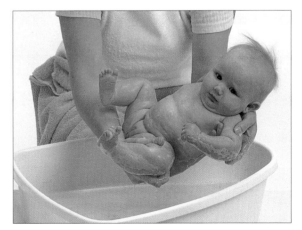

4 RINSE HER BOTTOM

Still supporting your baby across her chest, turn her around in the tub so that her face remains clear of the water. Rinse her lower back.

5 REMOVE HER FROM THE TUB

Keep one hand firmly on her shoulder and slide the other under her buttocks. Rotate her gently toward you so she faces upward as you lift her out of the tub.

73

DRYING YOUR BABY

Have an opened towel ready on the changing surface on which to place your baby. Soft cotton towels with integral hoods are specially manufactured for babies and are snug and warm. You don't have to use one but it is a good idea to reserve towels for your baby's exclusive use. You can warm your baby's towel on the radiator first, but avoid making it too hot.

As soon as you have removed your baby from the water, enfold her in the towel and cuddle her dry, smiling and talking with her all the while. This is a great opportunity to make your baby feel loved and secure.

Before you dress her, you should take pains to ensure that all her skin creases, particularly those in her thigh area, are dry. Any moisture left is likely to cause soreness and irritation – dampness can cause diaper rash.

If you are going to use baby powder, shake it onto your hands first so that your baby does not inhale any; do not use any on the diaper area. You also need to avoid excessive dryness. Baby oil in the bath water, or baby lotion for delicate areas, will protect her sensitive skin, and you can use waterproof ointments like petroleum jelly to guard against diaper rash.

Remember that your baby's skin is very sensitive, so use a soft towel and pat dry rather than rubbing.

" My baby is at her most delicious after her bath. I love to inhale the fragrance of her skin. "

1 Place your baby in the center of the towel

As soon as you take her out of the bath, wrap your baby in a warm towel. Gently fold one side over her but take care not to cover her face, as this may cause her to panic and start crying.

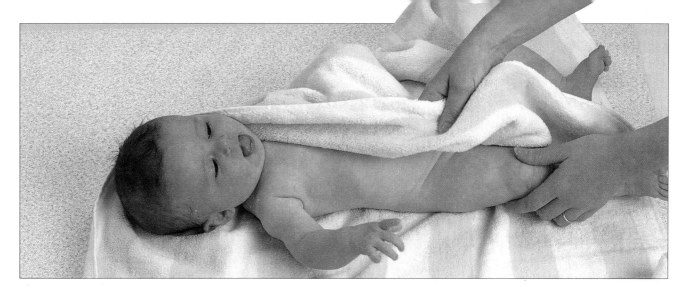

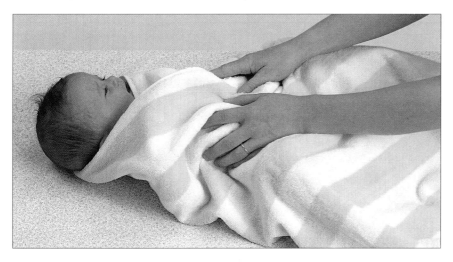

2 Pat her dry all over

Fold both sides over so that she is completely wrapped up, and gently pat her dry. Pay particular attention to the skin creases around her legs, her diaper area, under her arms, and around her neck.

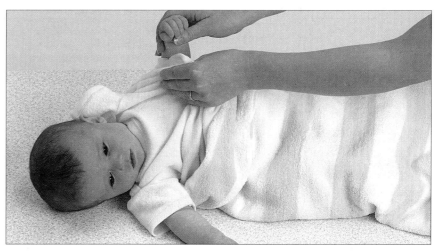

3 Keep your baby covered while you dress her

Begin to put on her clothes, keeping all exposed parts covered with the towel. This will help prevent her getting chilled. To be on the safe side, use a fresh clean towel for each bath.

DAILY CARE ROUTINES

In addition to cleaning and perhaps bathing your baby on a regular basis, there are a few areas of the body that need special attention. With newborns, you will have to attend to the umbilical cord and, if you have a baby boy, possibly his circumcised penis (see Cleaning a boy, pages 62-63).

Young babies have very sharp nails, and you will have to keep these short if you want to prevent your baby scratching himself. Babies can be prone to cradle cap, which may need attention. Finally, once your baby's teeth begin to arrive, it will be time to include tooth and gum care in your daily routine.

TAKING CARE OF THE UMBILICAL CORD STUMP

The umbilical cord was your baby's lifeline while he was in your uterus, linking him to your blood stream through the placenta. It provided him with oxygen, nutrients, antibodies and hormones, making him completely dependent on its supply.

When your baby takes his first breath, two momentous changes happen in seconds – his lungs inflate for the first time, and the blood flow is rerouted through the lungs, where previously it went through the umbilical cord. In an instant, your baby becomes able to survive independently.

Shortly after birth, the cord is clamped off and cut a few centimeters from the navel. There are no nerves in this area, so it is not a painful procedure for your baby. The cord

will gradually shrivel up, turn black and, within about ten days, fall off. Some parents, for sentimental or superstitious reasons, choose to keep the remnants of their baby's umbilical cord. In the meantime, however, it is susceptible to infection, particularly if it gets wet or dirty.

As long as your baby's umbilical cord stump remains attached, try and leave it open to the air, as this will make it dry, heal and fall off more rapidly.

While a slight discharge after the cord has withered is normal, call your doctor if the stump exudes pus or blood and the area around its base become inflamed – swollen, red and hot to the touch. These symptoms probably indicate an infection.

UMBILICAL HERNIA

You may notice that when your baby cries his navel protrudes. This swelling is called an umbilical hernia and is a very common occurrence among young babies.

Newborn babies have an opening in their abdominal walls through which blood vessels extend to the umbilical cord. After the cord is cut, stomach muscles grow and encircle the navel, but sometimes not completely. When your baby cries he puts pressure on these weak abdominal muscles, causing the intestines to push through to beneath the surface of his navel. The resulting bulge can be very small or the size of a golf ball.

Surgery is not necessary as the opening will usually close up by itself after a year or two.

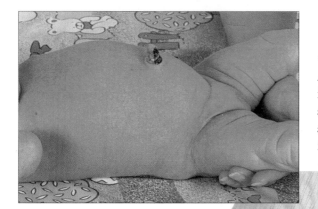

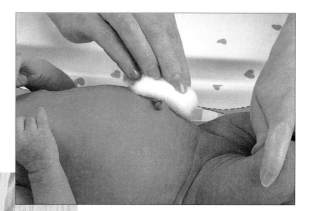

2 CLEANING THE STUMP
Rubbing alcohol will both keep the stump free of infection and make it fall off faster. Using a clean cotton ball moistened with rubbing alcohol, gently wipe the stump, the area around it, and the crevices of the navel.

1 EXPOSE THE STUMP TO AIR
The stump will dry and heal much faster if you expose it to air as much as possible. In particular, don't cover it with plastic pants and diapers and, if it does get wet, make sure it is thoroughly dried.

3 AFTER THE STUMP HAS FALLEN OFF
There may be a few spots of blood, and the wound will continue to heal. You should clean and dry it daily until the area is completely healed.

Taking care of your baby's hair and nails

Some babies are born with a full head of hair, but this is rare. It is more likely that your baby will have a sparse covering. Thick or thin, newborn hair is invariably shed after a couple of weeks – often a cause of concern for parents, but perfectly normal. Your baby may also have a covering of downy body hair, known as lanugo – this, too, will rub off within a couple of weeks.

Your baby's hair will need only simple care at first – wipe it down with a damp cloth or sponge (see Washing your baby's hair, pages 68-69), and brush it through with a soft comb. This should also guard against cradle cap. Cradle cap is a common but not serious condition that usually disappears after a couple of weeks, but you can get rid of it quickly by softening the scales with baby oil or specially manufactured cradle cap cream. Leave the cream or oil on overnight, then brush the scales off the next morning.

A newborn's nails are often quite long and you should trim them to stop him scratching himself. You may feel nervous about cutting such small nails, but there are some tips to help you. Cut the nails just after a bath, when they will be soft. Use blunt-ended nail scissors or baby nail clippers and follow the natural line of the finger, depressing the finger pad away from the nail. Your baby may put up some resistance when he gets older so you may want your partner to hold your baby's hand steady. If you are still worried about cutting, you can gently nibble off the nails – your mouth is more sensitive than a pair of scissors. Soft mittens on your baby's hands will prevent him scratching himself or irritating a dry skin condition.

Toenails tend to grow more slowly than fingernails but often excess skin encroaches onto the nail bed, making toenails difficult to trim. To avoid catching your baby's skin, cut toenails straight across. If you do draw some blood, blot with a tissue then dab some antiseptic ointment onto the area.

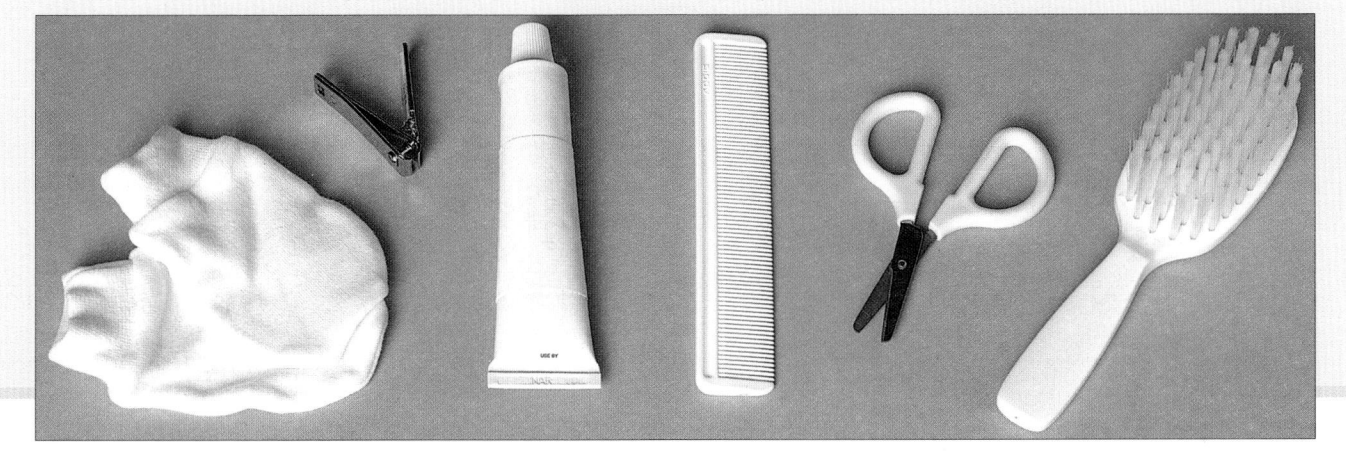

CRADLE CAP

• SIGNS OF CRADLE CAP

Some babies' skins produce an excess of grease resulting in yellow, scaly patches. This can irritate the skin leading to redness, particularly on the scalp.

• TREATING CRADLE CAP

If you like, soften the scales by massaging baby oil into the scalp. Leave overnight then brush the scales off the next morning with a soft brush.

NAILS

• CUTTING YOUR BABY'S NAILS

Sit your older baby in your lap so you can hold her securely. Use one hand to hold her fingers steady and the other to trim along the natural line with a pair of blunt-ended nail scissors.

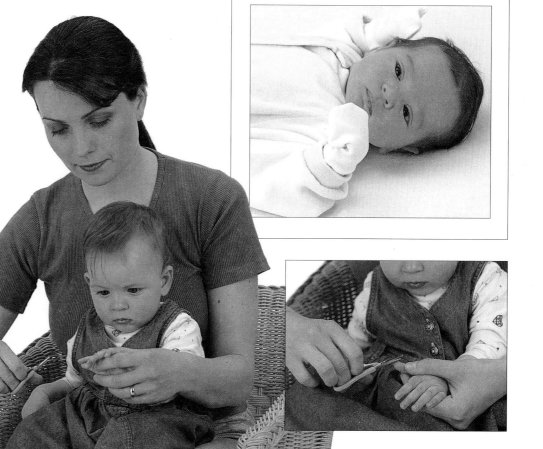

YOUNGER BABIES' NAILS

You can cover your baby's hands with a pair of soft mittens to prevent her scratching herself or irritating any dry skin condition she may have.

79

TEETHING

Your baby's first set of teeth are known as milk, primary or deciduous teeth. They amount to 20 in total and are usually all in place by the time your baby is two and a half years old. First teeth are very white which is one reason they are known as milk teeth.

At about six years of age your child will start to lose these teeth. They will gradually be replaced by a permanent set of 32 teeth.

Although the milk teeth are not permanent they are important because they allow your baby to begin to speak correctly and chew his food. Most importantly, they retain the space necessary for the permanent teeth.

TEETHING RINGS
Your baby will find safe relief from the pains of teething by chewing on soft, cooling, rubber teething rings.

Teeth are forming under the gums even before your baby is born and sometimes babies can be born with a milk tooth already in place. If this happens to your baby a pediatrican will check to see if it is securely fixed; if it is wobbly or if it interferes with breastfeeding it may have to be removed.

The first tooth usually appears at around five or six months of age but this can vary a great deal – anything between three to twelve months. The signs of teething will become apparent a few weeks before you see the first tooth. Your baby may start to drool a great deal and may become irritable as the teeth cut through his gums.

Below are a few suggestions to help make teething less painful for your baby.

OLD WIVES' TALES
Fever, vomiting and diarrhea are not signs of teething – even though some parents may think they are. These symptoms could be signs of serious illness in your baby and should always be investigated by your doctor.

WHEN TEETH APPEAR

Teeth erupt in upper and lower pairs and the first to appear are the two bottom front teeth. These are called the lower central incisors. They are followed by the two top front teeth, the upper central incisors. The next to appear are upper lateral incisors, the teeth either side of the upper central incisors. After this comes the second set of lower teeth, the lower central incisors. By the time your baby is a year old he should have a set of eight teeth, four on top and four on the bottom.

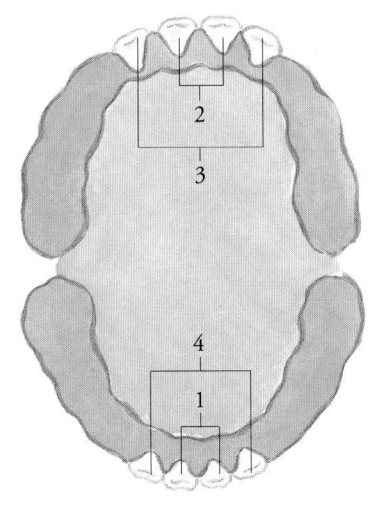

• DROOLING

Your baby will put his fingers, sometimes even his whole fist, into his mouth; this may be because he is teething and wants to relieve any tingling pain. Too much drooling can lead to a rash around your baby's chin and lips so make sure you wipe away any saliva. If a rash develops, apply petroleum jelly around the area.

• TEETHING BISCUITS

You can buy special baby rusks or teething biscuits for your baby to gnaw on, but a frozen bagel has the extra benefit of feeling cool against the gums and helping to reduce any swelling. Also, any bits that break off will soften so your baby can swallow them without harm.

• TEETHING RINGS

These special rubber toys contain a gel which you can make cool by placing in the refrigerator for a few hours. Your baby can put the teething ring in his mouth to massage and relieve any soreness around his gums.

• FIRST TEETH

Your baby's teeth are very sharp. Though many mothers successfully continue to breastfeed even when their babies have a mouthful, it is important to teach your baby not to bite.

CARING FOR YOUR BABY'S TEETH

Once your baby starts to teethe it is a good idea to get into a daily routine of tooth and gum care. If your baby has just one or two teeth you can add a drop of toothpaste to a clean handkerchief or small piece of gauze cloth and use this to wipe them. Use specially manufactured 'milk tooth' pastes, which contain low levels of fluoride. Avoid those that contain added sugar to make them more palatable. The sugar will only encourage plaque. If you can, discourage your baby from swallowing toothpaste.

When your baby has more than a few teeth you should start using a toothbrush. Your baby will not be able to clean her teeth properly for a few years yet, so you will have to take responsibility for this. Your baby will enjoy imitating you, however, so let her have her own brush to play with while she watches you brush your teeth. You should brush your baby's teeth every morning and every night before she goes to bed.

As well as daily cleaning you should limit the amount of sugary foods in your baby's diet. Never put your baby to bed with a bottle or let her suck endlessly on a bottle filled with milk or juice, as her teeth will be bathed in sugary fluid, which will encourage tooth decay. On the other hand, give her plenty of raw fruit and vegetables, which are naturally sweet and good to gnaw on.

Check frequently for signs of tooth decay and if you see any white, yellow, or brown spots on the teeth contact your dentist. After the age of three, when most of your child's milk teeth will have erupted, you should take her for regular dental check-ups.

FLUORIDE

Fluoride is a mineral which helps to fight tooth decay by strengthening the enamel coating on teeth. Most babies receive an adequate intake of fluoride through their local water supply, but fluoride levels vary from area to area, so you should check this with your local water department. If you find that your tap water is not adequately fluoridated, it is a good idea to consult your dentist for advice on fluoride supplements for your baby.

TOOTH SAFETY

Hard, sharp toys can damage a baby's teeth and gums. Only let your baby chew on suitably soft but firm objects.

• CLEAN ONE OR TWO BABY TEETH WITH A CLOTH

Gently wipe your baby's teeth and gums with a piece of gauze to get rid of the plaque, bacteria and acid, which cause tooth decay. Disposable cloth finger slips for this specific purpose are now being manufactured, so ask your local pediatric dentist where you can purchase these.

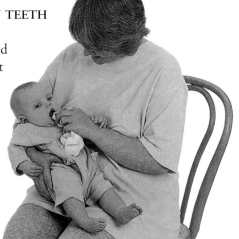

• FLOSS BETWEEN TOUCHING TEETH

Flossing helps to get rid of any built up plaque or food particles that can get lodged between the teeth. Hold a piece of dental floss between the thumbs and index fingers on both hands so that it is taut. Slowly ease the floss between the two touching teeth and gently slide it back and forth.

TOOTHBRUSHES

There are a wide variety of children's toothbrushes available. A brightly colored one will appeal to your child and he will be encouraged to use it.

Choose a toothbrush with soft, rounded bristles and change it every six to eight weeks, even if it doesn't look worn, because bacteria from your baby's mouth will accumulate on the brush.

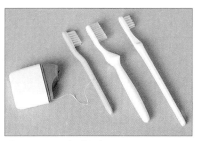

Once your baby has two or more teeth touching, use floss to clean between them.

• BRUSH YOUR BABY'S TEETH DAY AND NIGHT

Sit your baby on your lap with her back against you and carefully brush her teeth and gums. A gentle up and down motion will get rid of any plaque. Be careful when brushing the back of her mouth as your child might be frightened of gagging. Try and develop a routine of brushing in the morning and last thing at night.

AMUSING YOUR BABY

Your baby's play closely reflects her stage of mental, physical and sensory development. At first she will enjoy simply looking at moving objects and brightly colored toys. By two months of age she may begin swiping at things, particularly hanging musical mobiles, as her coordination improves. By three months of age your baby will be hitting and touching objects to get the feel of them – so she needs eye-catching objects that will stay within her reach. By five months of age she will want to put everything in her mouth, so you should choose your toys accordingly – small and light enough for her to manipulate, but chunky enough to prevent choking.

Bear in mind that your baby has a very short attention span. Don't waste money on expensive toys that she will quickly lose interest in – simple household objects such as keys or bits of tissue paper will do just as well.

When you do buy toys, choose bright, contrastingly colored ones that make noises; these will more easily capture a young baby's interest. Those that let her interact – with moving parts, levers and buttons – will exercise dexterity and teach her about cause and effect.

Remember – safety first: avoid toys that have sharp edges or removable bits that will catch fingers or get caught in throats. Always supervise your baby at play.

FUN IS WHERE YOU FIND IT
Something as simple as tissue paper can engage your baby's interest, and teach her about texture and pliability.

• HANGING TOYS

Different shapes strung across
a playseat, crib or playpen can
provide lots of fun for your
young baby.

• PUSH BUTTON TOYS

Once your child has a bit
of dexterity she will enjoy
pressing buttons and imitating
the actions of the adults
around her.

• A BASKETFUL OF TOYS

Babies have short attention spans
so a large number of simple toys,
rather than a few expensive ones,
are preferable. Babies also enjoy
putting objects into and taking them
out of containers.

• PULL TOYS

A perennial favorite,
moving, clacking toys
will encourage fine finger
movements on your
child's part, in
order to bring
them closer.

• MULTI-USE TOYS

Many toys can be used in
more than one way. Spools,
for example, can be placed one
on top of another or threaded
on a string and pulled.

PARENT AND CHILD ACTIVITIES

The times between those your baby spends sleeping, eating, crying and being washed and changed, can be the most rewarding for you both – playtime. In many ways, interacting with your child is more important than simply looking after his physical needs. It is vital for maintaining and enhancing the emotional bond between you, and can teach your baby about sociability and communication. Play will help your baby refine his movements, and improved coordination will assist in the development of his sensory and mental abilities. By responding to your baby's signals and encouraging his efforts, you build his confidence and self-belief, and reward and encourage his trust and love. You are your baby's first and most important teacher and play is an important teaching tool.

ENCOURAGE HIS RESPONSE
Even a simple toy, such as a rattle, can teach your child a great deal about sound, movement and texture. Any positive response on his part should be rewarded with smiles and laughter.

• HIDE AND SEEK

Your baby will enjoy watching you hide items under a towel or cushion, then retrieving them for you when you ask him where the 'lost' item is. Reward him with plenty of praise and cuddles.

• READING TOGETHER

Your baby will appreciate the sound of your voice and the idea of reading, even without total understanding. Point out and name objects and people. As she gets older, your baby will be able to point to them on request.

• USING TOYS

To make playtime more animated, give your baby's toys more character by providing movement and sound. This will help renew his interest in toys with which he may be bored.

• PEEK-A-BOO

This game is fun for both parent and baby. Use exaggerated facial and vocal expressions as you cover your face and reveal it again to your baby. Even though you've 'disappeared' only momentarily, your baby will be happy to welcome you back.

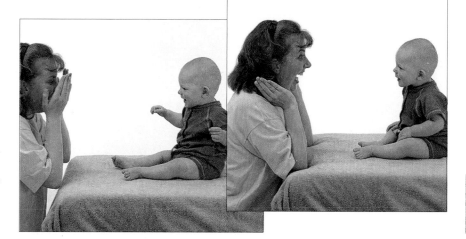

SIGNS OF ILLNESS

In an emergency situation you should call for medical help immediately. This is when your baby is unconscious or having difficulty breathing; is having convulsions; or is exhibiting unusual drowsiness, blue or very pale coloration, and abnormal floppiness. But there may be other times when you are unsure whether you should call the doctor. Following are some additional telltale signs that merit an immediate call.

The main warning symptoms are a raised or very low temperature – above 100.4°F (38°C) or below 95°F (35°C) (rectal readings); extended diarrhea (more than six hours); vomiting; loss of normally healthy appetite; listlessness; and prolonged crying that indicates to you that your baby may be in pain. Your doctor will appreciate any recorded observations about your baby's symptoms.

IF YOU THINK YOUR BABY IS ILL

Only in rare circumstances will your doctor make a house call, so if you have to make an office or hospital visit be prepared to take with you as much information as you can about your baby's condition, such as if and when he exhibited the symptoms listed above. A combination of symptoms is more serious than any one appearing singly.

A basic check to perform whenever you suspect your baby is sick is to take his temperature. Normal body temperature for a baby is 98.6°F (37°C). When the immune system is fighting infection, this will rise, producing a fever, while a serious drop indicates hypothermia. Take the temperature more than once, since it may be fluctuating. Do not take your baby's temperature orally in case he bites on and breaks the bulb – mercury is highly toxic. The most accurate temperature will be given by taking a rectal reading, though many parents prefer to use the underarm method. The least accurate is given by using a strip on the forehead.

A BABY'S PULSE

Parents are not normally required to take a baby's pulse except when recommended to do so by a doctor during illness.

The normal pulse rate for a young baby is quite high – between 100 and 160 beats per minute (bpm). A one-year-old's pulse slows to 100 to 120 bpm. You can take a baby's pulse by placing the palm of your hand over his chest by his left nipple, or you can take it at his wrist or just above the elbow.

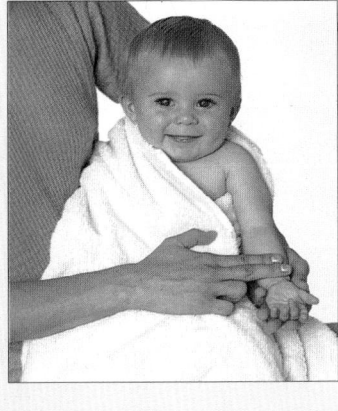

TAKING A PULSE
Count the number of heart beats in 15 seconds and multiply by four to get the bpm.

• TAKING AN UNDERARM TEMPERATURE

The underarm temperature is lower than internal body temperature by about 1°F (0.6°C). Despite this, taking your baby's temperature under his arm is the recommended method for everyday use. Cradle your baby in your lap. Wipe dry his armpit, shake down the thermometer and put the bulb into the fold of his armpit. Hold his arm flat against his side, and leave for three minutes.

• TAKING A RECTAL TEMPERATURE

The most accurate temperature is that given by a rectal reading, but many caregivers feel uncomfortable taking a temperature rectally. If your doctor suggests you take a rectal reading, use a rectal thermometer (with a short, round bulb), lubricate the tip with petroleum jelly and gently insert about one inch (25 mm) into the rectum. The recommended position is to lay your baby face down over your lap on a flat surface. Firmly press down the palm of one hand just above his buttocks to hold him still while you keep the thermometer in place for one minute to take a reading.

• TAKING AN EAR TEMPERATURE

A digital thermometer takes an infrared 'picture' of the eardrum to give a highly accurate and almost instantaneous reading. Lay your baby flat. Gently pull back the ear to straighten the ear canal, and carefully insert the tip of the thermometer until it fully seals the canal. Press and hold the activation button for one full second, and read off the temperature.

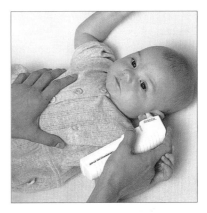

• TAKING A TEMPERATURE USING A FOREHEAD STRIP

Hold the strip across your baby's forehead, with a finger on either end, for about a minute. Though extremely easy to use, these strips are not very accurate, and are useful as a general guide only.

WHEN YOUR BABY IS ILL

After you have consulted with your doctor and determined the cause of your baby's illness, you will need to spend some time nursing your sick baby while he takes his course of medicine and regains his health.

It may be distressing as a parent to witness your baby in physical discomfort but you can help by providing a warm and caring environment. Ill babies in particular will want to be in very close contact with their mothers and will seek a lot more physical attention. If you are breastfeeding you may find your baby wanting to suckle simply for comfort.

If your baby has been vomiting, had diarrhea or a high temperature you need to

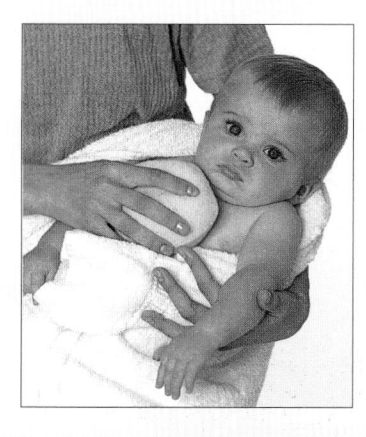

SPONGING YOUR BABY
Wrap your baby in a towel and sit him on your lap. Use a damp sponge soaked in boiled water cooled to a tepid temperature to wipe him down.

ensure he takes sufficient fluids to replace those he has lost.

A high fever can be dangerous, so you should try and bring down your baby's temperature. Make sure he is not wearing too many clothes, and ensure a good supply of fresh air to his room. Try sponging your baby down with tepid water. Check his temperature every ten minutes, and stop when it goes below 102°F (38.5°C).

In general, you will be following your doctor's instructions, and your main task may be to give your baby prescribed medications.

IMMUNIZATION

While the antibodies your baby has picked up from you through the placenta and breastfeeding will help him fight off many infections, there are a number of common childhood diseases to which he will be susceptible. Several of these can be dangerous and even life-threatening, so you should make sure your baby is vaccinated against the major childhood illnesses. These are diphtheria, pertussis (whooping cough), polio, measles, mumps, rubella (German measles), Hepatitis B, and haemophilus infections (which can cause meningitis and other diseases). A DTP injection will also protect your baby against tetanus. Some of the immunizations are taken together and several involve a course of shots.

IMMUNIZATION SCHEDULE

DIPHTHERIA, TETANUS, PERTUSSIS (DTP)
(this vaccine can be given in a safer acellular form – DTaP – after 15 months)
Given at 2, 4, and 6 months, and DTaP at 12 months and 4-6 years
POLIO
Given as oral polio vaccine at 2, 4 and 6 months, and at 4-6 years
MEASLES, MUMPS AND RUBELLA (MMR)
Given at 12-15 months, and either 4-6 years or 11-12 years
HEPATITIS B
Your doctor should recommend a schedule, but shots normally start at birth
HAEMOPHILUS
Given at 2, 4, 6 and 15 months

N.B. All are injections except for polio.

• **GIVING MEDICINE BY ORAL SYRINGE**
Cradle your baby in your arms and aim the tip of the syringe between her rear gums and cheek, avoiding the taste buds. Squirt the medicine slowly to avoid making her choke, and do not touch the back of the tongue with the syringe, since this could cause gagging.

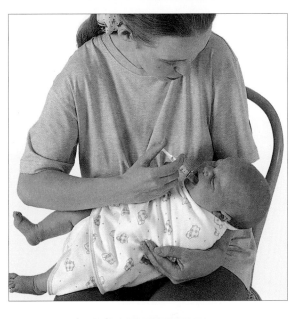

• **GIVING MEDICINE BY PACIFIER-STYLE SYRINGE**
The nipple-shaped tip allows your baby to suck while you express the medicine. Hold your baby in your lap, supporting his head in the crook of your arm. Put the tip of the syringe in his mouth as you would with a bottle and slowly press the plunger.

• **ADMINISTERING EYE DROPS**
Swaddle your baby to prevent wriggling, and lay her on her back. Tilt her head to one side, with the affected eye nearest your leg. Taking care not to touch the eye with the dropper, pull down her lower eyelid and squeeze the drops between it and the eye. You may need help to hold her head steady.

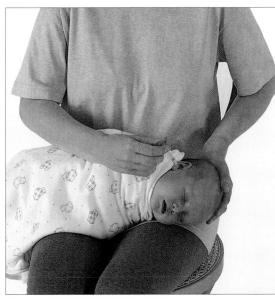

• **ADMINISTERING EAR DROPS**
Lay your baby on her side, with the affected ear uppermost. You need to drop the medicine down the ear canal, so pull back the lobe to straighten the canal, and put the dropper close to her ear. Hold your baby steady while the drops sink in – you can use cotton balls to soak up any leaks.

FIRST AID FOR BABIES

These basic instructions cannot substitute for proper training in first aid, but they could help save your baby's life. Always call for help in an emergency so that someone can contact the emergency services while you attend to your baby.

Your priorities are to check that her airway is clear, that she is breathing, and that her pulse is above 60 beats/min (120 is normal for a baby). If you suspect a spinal injury, do not twist your baby's head or body, and make her lie still.

ELECTRIC SHOCK

A crawling baby may stick her fingers in an unprotected outlet or chew on an electrical cord. A severe electric shock can stop her heart, interfere with breathing, cause shock, convulsions, and severe burns. Your priority is to break the circuit your baby is forming without getting electrocuted yourself.

Turn off the current or disconnect the plug, if possible. If not, stand on some dry non-conductive material such as wood or plastic and push your baby away using a chair leg or broom handle. As a last resort, pull your baby away by her clothes. Check for burns; if present, cover with a sterile dressing or plastic bag.

If your baby is unconscious, place her in the position shown on page 94. If she is not breathing or has no pulse, you will need to use rescue breathing or CPR (see page 95).

POISONING

Take extra care to keep hazardous substances out of reach, and make sure that medicines have child-proof caps. Suspect poisoning if your baby exhibits signs of vomiting, dizziness, convulsions, unconsciousness, and burns or discoloration around the mouth.

Contact your local poison control center or 911. Try and find out what she took, how much and how long ago, so that you can inform the doctor or paramedics. Keep a sample of any vomit she produces – but don't try and make her sick. You can give her milk or water. If she is unconscious but breathing, put her in the position shown on page 94.

If your baby is not breathing, try rescue breathing (see page 95), but wipe her face and breathe through a cloth.

BLEEDING

Severe blood loss could send your baby into shock (see page 94), and must be dealt with promptly. The basic rules are to apply direct pressure to the wound and raise the injured part above the level of the heart.

Lay your baby down and keep the injured part raised. If something is in the wound apply pressure on both sides, but do not remove the foreign body. Expose the wound by cutting away clothing if necessary, and apply pressure with a clean dressing.

For a severe wound (e.g. one that is spurting blood, indicating that an artery is cut) apply pressure for at least ten minutes, then put on a pressure bandage. If blood leaks through, do not replace the dressing but wrap more gauze around the first dressing.

CHOKING

This is one of the most common causes of death in babies as they try to put everything in their mouths.

If you suspect your child is choking but she can still cry and cough, pat her back gently. Only attempt the sequence below if she is conscious but cannot cry, cough or breathe, or if she is making high-pitched noises and is coughing very weakly.

If you do the following but still cannot feel a pulse, you must be prepared to perform CPR (see page 95).

1 GIVE FOUR BACK BLOWS

Hold your baby with her head below her body, face down along your forearm, which is resting on your thigh. Firmly hold her jaw between your thumb and fingers. Using the heel of your hand, strike her sharply four times between her shoulder blades.

2 GIVE FOUR CHEST THRUSTS

If she still doesn't cry, sandwich her between both your arms then turn her face up along one arm. Support her against your thigh. Place the ring finger of the hand supporting her chest on the breastbone just below the nipples; place the next two fingers alongside. Remove your ring finger and with two fingers only compress the breastbone ½ to 1 inch (1½ to 2½ cm), then allow it to return to normal. Compress four times in all. Continue until the object is coughed up or your baby becomes unconscious.

IF YOUR BABY LOSES CONSCIOUSNESS

Place your baby on her back on the floor and perform a foreign body check.

Hold your baby's tongue and lower jaw between your thumb and fingers. Lift the jaw upward. If you see an object, remove it. Otherwise, slide the little finger of your other hand into her mouth to the base of the tongue. If you see the item now, use a hooking action to try and remove it, being careful not to push the object in further.

IF YOUR BABY REMAINS UNCONSCIOUS AND NOT BREATHING

Open the airway by tilting her forehead back and lifting her chin. Check if she is breathing by looking to see if the chest is moving, listening for sounds, or by feeling air on your cheek. If not, cover her mouth and nose with your mouth and gently give her two breaths (see page 95), then give four back blows and four chest thrusts. Repeat this sequence over and over until she breathes or help arrives.

RESCUE BREATHING AND CPR

A variety of accidents and emergency situations can cause your baby to fall unconscious and stop breathing. If too little oxygen gets into the blood, brain damage or heart failure may result.

If you find your baby lying still and suspect something is wrong, yell for help so another adult can contact the emergency services. You must resuscitate your baby if she is not breathing or has no pulse.

Check for unconsciousness by tapping or scratching the soles of your baby's feet and calling her name. If she doesn't respond, turn her onto her back immediately. Try to roll your baby as a unit to prevent making any injuries worse. Support her all along the length of her body as you turn her onto her back. You then should perform rescue breathing and, if necessary, CPR.

IF YOUR BABY SHOULD VOMIT

An unconscious baby may vomit while you are helping her to breathe. It is important that vomit does not get into your baby's lungs. Quickly turn your baby's head and body to the side and wipe away any vomit. Then continue rescue breathing.

SHOCK

Blood pressure drops dangerously low during this life-threatening condition. Warning signs are cold, sweaty skin; a greyish tinge around the lips and nails; shallow breathing and unconsciousness.

Call for emergency help immediately. Lay your baby on a coat or blanket, turn her head to the side, in case she vomits, and raise her feet about eight inches (20 centimeters). Loosen any clothing and keep her warm but not hot.

HOLDING AN UNCONSCIOUS BABY

If your baby is unconscious but breathing, and there is no sign of fracture, hold her in this position until help arrives.

Cradle her in your arms with her head tilted slightly back. This keeps her airway open and allows liquids to drain from her mouth.

DROWNING

A baby who slips under the water in a bath – even if only an inch or so of water covers her mouth and nose – may drown in a couple of minutes.

If you find your baby in water, lift her out immediately and hold her so her head is lower than her body. This will help prevent water, or vomit if she throws up, getting into her lungs. If she is unconscious, place her in the position shown left while you call the emergency services. If she is not breathing you must perform rescue breathing. Water in the lungs will mean you will have to breathe more firmly than usual to get the lungs inflated.

RESCUE BREATHING

1 OPEN THE AIRWAY AND CHECK FOR BREATHING
Gently supporting her forehead with one hand, place a finger (not the thumb) of your other hand under her jaw. Tilt her head gently back and lift the chin at the same time. See if you can detect any movement in the chest or feel any breath against your cheek.

2 GIVE TWO SLOW BREATHS
If there is no sign of breathing, open your mouth wide and take a breath. Cover your baby's nose and mouth with your mouth and slowly breathe out for about one to two seconds. Look along her chest to make sure it rises when you breathe into your baby and watch to see her chest fall when you stop. Repeat.

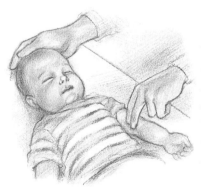

3 CHECK THE PULSE
To see if your baby's heart is beating, feel along the inside of her upper arm, between the elbow and the shoulder. Press gently with your index and middle fingers for five seconds. If there is no pulse give CPR. If there is, continue rescue breathing, checking her pulse every minute, until she is breathing or help arrives.

CPR (CARDIOPULMONARY RESUSCITATION)

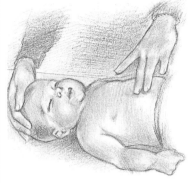

1 LOCATE THE COMPRESSION POINT
Kneel alongside your baby. Hold her forehead with one hand and position the index finger of the other just under the midpoint of an imaginary line running between her nipples. Place the next two fingers underneath. Raise the index finger. You should be just below the breastbone.

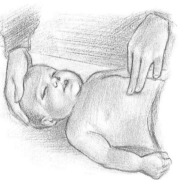

2 COMPRESS THE CHEST FIVE TIMES
Using your two fingers and bending your elbow, push down sharply ½ to 1 inch (1½ to 2½ cm), then release. Use a steady down and up pace. Give five compressions, counting aloud 'one, two, three, four, five' very quickly as you do so.

3 GIVE ONE SLOW BREATH
After five compressions, give one slow breath lasting one to two seconds. Repeat this ten times. Recheck the pulse for five seconds. If there is no pulse, continue with one breath and then cycles of compressions and a breath. Once your baby starts breathing, stop breaths and CPR and hold her as shown on page 94, checking her pulse every minute.

INDEX

ACKNOWLEDGMENTS

Carroll & Brown would very much like to thank:

Donald Schiff, M.D. for his pediatric advice

Children's World for the use of their equipment

Freemans for the use of their clothing

Rachel Attfield for hair and make-up

David Murray for additional photography

Arthur Barham, Sid Sideris and Neil Geugan for photographic assistance